A crisis, such as a pandemic, always leaves us changed for good or ill and, in the process, tests the values and priorities of the heart. For the Christian, a question always haunts: am I living in tune with the superficial herd spirit of the times or with the spirit of the divine depths, known as 'wisdom'? To help glimpse an answer, the letter of James should be read and so should Joel Huffstetler's reflections on it. Accessible, gracefully provocative and drenched in the reckless mercy of God, these meditations help us imagine what a true ambassador for Jesus Christ might say and do, how they might listen and how they might love.

Mark Oakley
Dean, St. John's College, University of Cambridge

Practical Faith and Active Love: Meditations on the Epistle of James is a 'game plan for life.' Joel Huffstetler has a passion for God, teaching, and also a love of Sport. These meditations on the wisdom of James reflect this. Fr. Joel emphasizes the practical teachings of James and their relevance for twenty-first century living.

As Athletic Director at The University of Tennessee, I had the privilege of working with Coach Pat Summitt for three decades. I have often been asked what made her a great coach and I always answer that she was a great teacher and understood the importance of relationships and communication.

Fr. Joel and Pat both share these characteristics. He is also a great teacher and communicator, and in this book he guides us through the Epistle of James with the touch of a seasoned pastor.

Joan Cronan, Athletic Director Emeritus
University of Tennessee

These short and elegant meditations on an often overlooked part of the New Testament by a first rate scholar priest offer much food for thought as we try to relate the Bible to our own often troubled world. Drawing on an extensive pastoral ministry as well as modern scholarship, Fr. Huffstetler succeeds in offering comfort, challenge and resources for the Christian life.

The Revd Canon Professor Mark D. Chapman
Professor of the History of Modern Theology, University of Oxford

PRACTICAL FAITH & ACTIVE LOVE

MEDITATIONS ON THE EPISTLE OF JAMES

JOEL W. HUFFSTETLER

APOCRYPHILE
PRESS

Apocryphile Press
1700 Shattuck Ave #81
Berkeley, CA 94709
www.apocryphilepress.com

Copyright © 2020 by Joel W. Huffstetler
Printed in the United States of America
ISBN 978-1-949643-79-4 | paper
ISBN 978-1-949643-80-0 | ePub

Please join our mailing list at
www.apocryphilepress.com/free
We'll keep you up-to-date on all our new releases,
and we'll also send you a FREE BOOK.
Visit us today!

For Debbie

CONTENTS

FOREWORD

"There is nothing in the Epistle of James that is not directly relevant to our lives." So writes Joel Huffstetler in one of his probing meditations that comprise this commendable book. Several times, we are reminded that James is not only a moral theologian but also a practical theologian—an early Christian writer, possibly Jesus's own brother, who has given us the only New Testament writing that can rightly be called "wisdom literature." Like the Old Testament book of Proverbs or other Jewish writings such as Ecclesiasticus, also known as the Wisdom of Jesus ben Sirach, and the Wisdom of Solomon, the Epistle of James consists mostly of sayings and proverbs, or short snippets of reflection on topics like riches and poverty, speech and anger, faith and works, patience and hope. From start to finish, these teachings of James resonate with our own—with everyone's—life experience. This is what makes them eminently—and profoundly—practical. They embody universal wisdom, especially that which comes to us through the Hebrew Scriptures and other Jewish writings from antiquity.

Wisdom teachings are typically succinct, direct, and forthright. They offer simple, insightful advice, but not because of some "know-it-all" arrogance, but because they grow out of life's experiences—out of a life deeply lived. They stem from people who have experienced the ups and downs of life, but who have taken the time to reflect on these experiences—and to learn from them. They are lessons about life that are drawn from life. But more than simply offering advice, James's teachings, like those of his wise predecessors, have an ethical dimension. They have an inescapable moral goal—the shaping of our lives in a direction toward what is good and beneficial, what is ultimately constructive and uplifting, in short, what is fully human. This is what Huffstetler means when he reminds us that James is a moral theologian—and a preacher.

These meditations on James grow out of deep, extensive pastoral experience in which the Bible is regarded and experienced as singularly formative in shaping the life of faith and the Christian communities in which such lives are nourished. In constructing these meditations, Huffstetler has drawn on a wide variety of scholarly voices drawn from the vast commentary tradition on the Epistle of James. Especially striking is the rich diversity of these voices, both women and men, scholars from many different church traditions, but other literary voices as well. Rather than simply stringing these commentary voices together and abjectly yielding to their expertise, Huffstetler has interwoven them with his own experienced voice as a reflective pastor. What emerges are brief but insightful meditations that exemplify the irresistible appeal of Scripture as believers and their communities deal with life's crises.

The social and political upheaval of 2020, compounded by a pandemic that has profoundly altered our routine patterns of life, provides the broader context in which these meditations have been prepared and delivered. As we all have sought markers to guide us through this fog of uncertainty, Huffstetler shows, once again, the value of Holy Scripture and such classics as *The Book of Common Prayer* in nurturing our souls even as we try to preserve our physical health.

Carl R. Holladay
Charles Howard Candler Professor Emeritus of New Testament
Candler School of Theology
Emory University

PREFACE

It has long been my contention that the Epistle of James is the most practical book of the Bible. A relatively brief document by biblical standards, James's 'epistle' is a collection of tried and true wisdom sayings both thoroughly Jewish and at the same time reflective of the Greco-Roman moralists. For years I have had the desire to work through the contents of the epistle systematically and then offer a series of practical reflections on this most practical of books. With the temporary suspension of in-person worship in 2020 due to safety protocols in response to COVID-19, the opportunity presented itself. The meditations that follow are revised versions of a series of informal reflections offered in the context of Noonday Prayer services which were live-streamed on Facebook.

This book is not a comprehensive commentary on the epistle. A gracious plenty of commentaries is already available. Instead, this series of meditations first offered in the context of worship, and now in print, seeks to remind interested readers of the timeless wisdom contained within the Epistle of James. The backdrop to this particular set of reflections is the COVID-19 pandemic, and the social protests first prompted by the deaths of Ahmaud Arbery and George Floyd—protests which continue to this day. The contents of James are relevant to any time, place, and circumstance, and the pastoral reflections on the epistle offered in this book will continue to apply going forward.

We cannot know for sure the identity of James. The attribution of the epistle to James the brother of Jesus is both a widespread and defensible assertion but cannot be proven. This treatment allows for the possibility that the epistle does go back to that James. The Epistle of James is a 'letter' in name only. The author has made use of the literary form in order to convey his collection of wisdom material in an accessible way. No firm date can be attached to the letter. In introductory comments regarding the document, Sophie Laws notes: "The very general nature of its contents makes it difficult to attach it positively to a specific time and place."[1] That said, the author's intended audience does seem to be a specific congregation. As Laws puts it: "The author presupposes a real audience."[2]

James's familiarity with wisdom literature both Jewish and Greco-Roman is impressive. Drawing widely from the literary resources available to him, James uses his letter to promulgate universally recognized virtues and to caution against universally recognized vices. Though the document contains only two specific references to Jesus by name (1:1; 2:1), there are distinct echoes of the Jesus tradition—including the Sermon on the Mount—throughout the letter.

Readers familiar with the wisdom texts of the Old Testament and the Apocrypha will find in James a continuation of the wisdom tradition into the Christian era. Carl Holladay notes that James is "...the one New Testament writing that can rightly be called Christian Wisdom literature."[3] In summarizing the scope and aim of the Epistle of James and its continuing relevance to contemporary church life, Luke Timothy Johnson states: "James claims neither novelty nor depth. But no reader can mistake its lively voice or moral passion. Traditional teaching is given vibrancy in this exhortation to practical faith and active love."[4]

Joel W. Huffstetler
Rector, St. Luke's Episcopal Church
Cleveland, Tennessee
23 December 2020

INTRODUCTION

Before I met Fr. Joel Huffstetler in person, I knew him to be a writer. While browsing at Accent On Books, an independent bookstore in Asheville, North Carolina, several years ago, I discovered Fr. Joel's very helpful guide on the Windsor Report. Here was a parish priest with the additional discipline of teaching and writing for publication. Fr. Joel had my personal admiration long before I had the pleasure to know him as a colleague in East Tennessee.

On each of my visits to St. Luke's, Cleveland, I always depart with a deep sense that St. Luke's is a teaching parish, with a teaching priest who invites the parish community to go deep—into Scripture, into prayer, into embodying the Faith.

I am writing this on January 1, 2021, with the very difficult Plague year 2020 just past. In March, traditional parish church life for all of us was wildly disrupted. How do we stay connected if we cannot physically gather in person? Now, we know we have learned new ways of using technology to remain a body of believers. And as Fr. Joel quotes me in these meditations as saying, we all returned to what we do best.

Fr. Joel possesses many gifts and there are many things he

does well. But at his best, I believe him to be a teacher and a writer. He is gifted in communicating the Gospel in practical and clear and effective ways. So, it is not surprising to me that he gave the parish church in Cleveland such a good gift with these practical and wise teachings on the Epistle of James.

In reading these meditations on the wisdom of James, I was reminded of Fr. James Otis Sargent Huntington, who helped found the Order of the Holy Cross in the late 1800s. He once said, "Love must act as light must shine forth and fire must burn." For Huntington, his life as a monk was integrated in prayer *and* action.

We know that it is Divine Grace that restores us to God, not our imperfect works. Yet, our response to that Divine Grace does act and shine and burn. Fr. Joel, through careful reading of commentators and his own pastoral reflections, shows how James invites us to practical action in response to Divine Grace.

My prayer for 2021 and beyond is that these meditations on the Epistle of James will find a wide readership, and I believe they will. Just as Fr. Joel suggests the genius of James is how practical it is, how it reads "as if we are sitting with a pastor from the ancient church and receiving instruction" so also with these meditations. As reader, you are sitting with a scholar pastor and his parish church, receiving instruction on the enduring wisdom of the Faith given to us through the Crucified and Risen Christ.

The Right Rev. Brian L. Cole
Bishop of East Tennessee
The Feast of the Holy Name of Our Lord Jesus Christ

PRACTICAL FAITH AND ACTIVE LOVE

JAMES 1:1-4 • 11 JUNE 2020

¹James, a servant of God and of the Lord Jesus Christ, To the twelve tribes in the Dispersion: Greetings. ²My brothers and sisters, whenever you face trials of any kind, consider it nothing but joy, ³because you know that the testing of your faith produces endurance; ⁴and let endurance have its full effect, so that you may be mature and complete, lacking in nothing.

The Letter of James fits into a genre known as wisdom literature. Proverbs is the great example of a wisdom text in the Hebrew Scriptures. And in the Apocrypha, dating from the inter-testamental period, is a wisdom text called Ecclesiasticus, sometimes referred to as Sirach. The Epistle of James carries forward the wisdom tradition into the Christian era.

James has a conversational tone. In reading through James, it is as if we are sitting with a pastor from the ancient church and receiving instruction regarding the practical aspects of faith. It *is* practical. Every line in James can be put to practical use in daily living, and the wisdom contained in James is just as relevant and useful to *us* as it was in the first century.

In 1:2-4 James mentions "trials" and "testing." In 1:2 we read: "...whenever you face trials of any kind...." James's wording here is intentional. "Trials" is in the plural. We all face different kinds of trials in life, different levels of testing. In referencing trials of "any kind" James asserts that whatever testing we endure, the journey through such times can lead us into a deeper maturity in the faith. For James, times of trial, times of testing, are a matter of when, not if, and when we face these inevitable times of testing James would have us draw on our faith for both wisdom and strength. Our faith is meant to help us put times of trial in perspective. It is our faith that gives us the will and the resources to move through such times, to face up to them without being overwhelmed.

Then in 1:3: "...the testing of your faith produces endurance...." The Greek for "endurance" has an active sense and does not connote mere passivity. To endure is actively to take on times of trial and testing. In commenting on the meaning of the word here in its context, Sophie Laws writes that endurance indicates: "...an active steadfastness in, [rather] than passive submission to, circumstances."[1] Endurance carries with it a connotation of active steadfastness, not passivity—merely holding on tight and riding it out.

The Epistle of James was written to help us deal with, make sense of, and learn from our trials, our times of testing. Of course, the path leading towards endurance is a journey. There will be successes and setbacks along the way. It is a lifetime's journey to grow more and more into maturity as people of faith. To be sure, endurance can be a gradual and, indeed, a painful acquisition. The journey into spiritual maturity, the winding path that leads us into deeper faith can be achingly gradual and deeply painful—and yet....

In this moment in our history there is much pain, anger,

frustration, and uncertainty. We are experiencing a collective fatigue in our culture. There is a weariness that comes with this season of trials. We are in the midst of a time of testing in our lives as individuals, as people of faith, and as a nation. Indeed, we are experiencing a time of trials the likes of which few of us middle-aged and younger have ever seen. We have a public health crisis to deal with, as well as protests calling for significant and lasting social change. Without doubt, we are *in* a time of testing, a season of trials.

In the biblical tradition, there is a history of framing times of trial, times of testing, in terms of a refining fire. In his commentary on James, Peter H. Davids writes: "The process of testing faith is like the tempering of steel: the heat, rather than destroying the steel, makes it stronger."[2] James readily acknowledges and in no way seeks to minimize the potential severity of trials. There will be times when we are sorely tested. James offers us wisdom to meet such times with faith, with perseverance, and with hope that we will emerge stronger, more mature, and more compassionate. However gradual and painful the journey, ultimately we are meant to come through our trials stronger for them.

James 1:3-4 reads: "...you know that the testing of your faith produces endurance; and let endurance have its full effect, so that you may be mature and complete, lacking in nothing." Many of us, surely most of us, are longing for a calmer, more peaceful time. But peace with justice. Numerous times over the last number of weeks I have thought how wonderful 'normal' would seem right now. Currently, there is nothing boring to me about normal! And yet, upon reflection, we know that, in reality, it is in times of struggle, times of challenge—it is in times when we are pushed out of our comfort zones that we grow in endurance and maturity and are edged forward in our faith journey. The maturity that James imagines comes in large part from what we learn from setbacks experienced in the midst of times of trial. It takes time and *patience* to get through these periods. It takes time to gain perspective, and yet, with the benefit of sufficient time and its accompanying hindsight, we recognize that it is through times of testing that we are pushed forward in the journey to maturity.

This is a momentous time in our lives. We are living in a time of challenge on numerous important fronts and, to be sure, we are in the midst of a much needed season of substantive social change. There is no question that we are living in and through a period that history will come to see as a season of lastingly significant change in our culture. For many, what we are experiencing is unsettling on numerous fronts. And yet, this can also be a time of hope, trusting that, having experienced this season, over time we as a culture, we as a church, and we as individuals will emerge the better for it.

James did not write his letter in a spiritual vacuum. James knew full well the reality of trials. He knew full well what it means to be tested. The Epistle of James was written in the first century out of a Jewish religious and cultural milieu. James had lived his entire life amidst the reality of an occupying foreign power, Rome. He had experienced the push/pull of the Judaism he had known evolving into a new expression of faith which would come to be called Christianity. Just imagine the challenge of wanting to be true to one's Jewish heritage and yet coming to understand that the Messiah *has come*, history has turned, in the person of Jesus.

Though we cannot prove it—no one can prove it—tradition holds that our author, James, is St. James of Jerusalem, the brother of Jesus. This James came to be in a position of leadership over the church in Jerusalem. So, if in fact our author is Jesus's brother, then James knew all too well the trials that Jesus had experienced—betrayal, arrest, mock trial, and crucifixion. The Epistle of James is not written in a spiritual vacuum. Our author speaks to the issues of trials and testing, endurance and the journey to maturity, with integrity, and from a deep well of experience.

In 1:4 we read: "...and let endurance have its full effect, so that you may be mature and complete, lacking in nothing." One of the leading scholars on the Epistle of James is Ralph Martin, and in his commentary he writes that maturity and completeness are meant to lead us to: "...the coherence of faith and works, i.e., in conduct."[3] James will go on to say in 1:22: "But be doers of the word, and not merely hearers...."

James writes squarely in the tradition of wisdom literature. The Epistle of James is full of ancient, time-tested, practical spiritual counsel that equips us to meet the moment that is now. Luke Timothy Johnson, one of the great Bible scholars of our time, writes in introducing the epistle: "James exhorts his readers to action consonant with conviction."[4] Johnson goes on to say that the exhortation that James offers us is to: "...practical faith and active love."[5] Amen.

OUR TIME AND PLACE

JAMES 1:16-18 • 18 JUNE, 2020

¹⁶**Do not be deceived, my beloved.** ¹⁷**Every generous act of giving, with every perfect gift, is from above, coming down from the Father of lights, with whom there is no variation or shadow due to change.** ¹⁸**In fulfillment of his own purpose he gave us birth by the word of truth, so that we would become a kind of first fruits of his creatures.**

James acknowledges in 1:2-3 that there are times of trial, there are periods of testing in our lives, but in 1:17 he makes it clear that *God* does not ever tempt us to evil. There is an important theological distinction to be made between times of trial, times of testing, and intentionality on the part of God in tempting us to evil. James is adamant: God *does not* tempt us to evil.

The term "Father of lights" in 1:17 is unique to James. While there are similar designations for God involving "Father," "Father of lights" occurs nowhere else in the Bible except here and is a clear homage to the Judeo-Christian tradition of monotheism, to Genesis and its stories of creation. For James,

God is the "Father of lights," the God of the monotheistic Hebrew Scriptures, in whom there is *no* variation or shadow due to change.

During the course of a day we see variations in light. At different times we see variations in light cast by the sun and the moon, and the stars are *more* or *less* visible to us at different times. There are variations in our experiences of light, but the "Father of lights," the divinity behind it all, is timeless, and does not change.

If we zoom out for a moment from the details 1:16-18, we remember that James carries forward into the Christian era the genre of wisdom literature. In his wisdom book, James makes the point early on that the essence of divinity—God's nature—is constant, consistent, and trustworthy. "Every *generous* (emphasis mine) act of giving, with every *perfect* (emphasis mine) gift, is from above, coming down from the Father of lights, with whom there is no variation or shadow due to change." Divinity, James is telling us, is the same yesterday, today, and forever.

In mid-life I have developed a real passion for art, particularly paintings. I have no formal training in this area. I have no training in Art History, and I have even less training in the practice of painting. But in mid-life I have acquired a real passion for the joy derived from an appreciation of fine art and, like many others, find myself drawn to the work of the great French impressionist, Claude Monet. In preparing this meditation I thought about Monet's fascination with Rouen Cathedral, which he painted *thirty times* in different light: the same building, in the same space, but thirty different interpretations based on the interplay between the cathedral and the changing light. I am particularly interested as well in Monet's paintings of London's Houses of Parliament. He produced three paintings of the Houses of Parliament over a three-year period at the turn of the twentieth century—three different representations of the Houses of Parliament—again, a study of changing light. The same building, in the same space, looks noticeably and significantly different based on changing light.

In our home, our favorite painting, the one I would save in a fire, is *Exuberance*. It is by a contemporary artist named Brenda Orcutt. The painting is marked by a riot of color, but in the end there is an order to it—a pattern emerges. The colors of *Exuberance* are varied and beautiful, and—to my eyes—their interplay with each other is spectacular. It is no exaggeration to say that every evening, before I turn in, I spend time looking at that painting—literally every evening of the week. I gaze upon it to enjoy, not 'study' it, but what I find in my enjoyment of the piece is that every time I look at it I see something new. Every time I take in *Exuberance* I notice a placement of color that I have not seen before, or an interplay of colors that previously escaped my attention—and I see the painting daily. The painting hangs in the same space, yet it always offers something new.

The Judeo-Christian tradition is clear, from Genesis, to James, to now, that we worship one God, who was, and is, and ever shall be. The Divine essence is constant, but change is inevitable for *us*. Culture is constantly changing. Cultural norms are constantly evolving. This was, and is, and ever shall be. The essence of God remains constant, but how we interpret God, how we understand God, how we 'see' God is always evolving based on the lens of culture. We have no other lens through which to see God for ourselves other than our own historical context, our own cultural norms and values. We approach conversation about God through the 'lens' of language. We have no other choice but to approach theology primarily through the lens of our own time and place. However much we may value Holy Scripture and Christian tradition, we cannot do other than engage in theological reflection and discourse as occupants of our own time and place. And like us, our ancestors had no other choice. Theological understanding is, always and inevitably, culturally conditioned.

The Book of Common Prayer (1979) states plainly that Holy Eucharist is "...the principal act of worship on the Lord's Day...."[1] Upon the 1979 Prayer Book becoming normative for worship in the Episcopal Church, the liturgy of Morning Prayer as a public act of worship on Sundays almost disappeared until earlier this year when, in response to COVID-19, social distancing became the norm. Suddenly Morning Prayer is back in countless parishes as the principal act of worship after a forty-year absence. The *moment* has dictated this. All the scholarly work, all the careful, calculated planning that went into the 1979 Prayer Book naming Holy Eucharist as the principal act of worship did not anticipate the global pandemic of 2020, and the sudden cessation of in-person public worship. Morning Prayer is back because of our time and place. We cannot do other than engage in theological reflection and discourse through the lens of culture of a certain time and place—our time and place. Thus, while we believe that God's essence is constant, unchanging, how we interpret that essence, what we can 'see' of God evolves and shifts over time in the changing light of culture.

In 1:18 we read: "...the word of truth...." The 'truth' is the ultimate aim of spirituality—the search for truth, the knowledge and guidance of truth. But our understanding of truth is always partial. We can never, this side of eternity, know fully the mind of God. Our search for truth, as passionate as it may be, is ongoing because our understanding of truth is always partial, always evolving. In 1 Corinthians 13:9-10 Paul writes: "For we know only in part, and we prophesy only in part; but when the complete comes, the partial will come to an end." The "complete" here is the kingdom in its fullness. Paul continues in 13:12: "For now we see in a mirror, dimly, but then we will see face to face. Now I know only in part; then I will know fully...." Earlier in his life Paul had an experience of the risen Christ, and thus had his life completely turned around in a moment of divine intervention and revelation. Even so, Paul articulates that even his, and certainly our, understanding of truth is always partial, and thus our search for truth is always ongoing. For Paul, as for James, the essence of the nature of God is constant but our *experience* of God, our understanding of Divine Love, is always evolving and is guided by the power and presence of the Holy Spirit.

Karl Barth, arguably the greatest biblical theologian of the twentieth century, observed with regard to sermon preparation that the preacher should have the Bible in one hand and a newspaper in the other. During the preparation of this meditation, in light of all that is happening with regard to social protests, I was reminded how often in this country's history Christian ministers stood in Christian pulpits and used select Bible passages to defend the institution of slavery. This is unimaginable to us now, but it occurred in our country in another time, in another cultural moment. That moment is past, and, to be sure, a new day, a new cultural moment is dawning right before our eyes.

"Every generous act of giving, with every perfect gift, is from above, coming down from the Father of lights, with whom there is no variation or shadow due to change." Divine Love is the same yesterday, today, and forever, yet through the Holy Spirit is always drawing humanity forward, drawing us closer to God's desire for the human family to see each other not as 'other,' but as sisters and brothers (cf. John 16:12-13). In his commentary on James, Luke Timothy Johnson writes regarding 1:17 that it is one of the "noblest" theological statements in the New Testament.[2] Johnson's insightful claim leads me to think of another of the noblest statements in the New Testament, 1 John 4:16: "...God is love, and those who abide in love abide in God, and God abides in them." Amen.

THE IMPORTANCE OF LISTENING

JAMES 1:19-21 • 25 JUNE 2020

¹⁹You must understand this, my beloved: let everyone be quick to listen, slow to speak, slow to anger; ²⁰for your anger does not produce God's righteousness. ²¹Therefore rid yourselves of all sordidness and rank growth of wickedness, and welcome with meekness the implanted word that has the power to save your souls.

In preparing for this meditation, I had memories of pastoral appointments over the years during which, after about an hour, I realized that other than an occasional nod of my head and the occasional "Go on..." I had hardly said a word for the entire time. This has happened numerous times over the years. And typically, my having listened to them intently for an hour, upon leaving these parishioners have said in so many words: "This has been so helpful. Thank you very much." In reality, all I had done was listen.

Having reached my 30th year of ordained ministry, I have noticed something in recent years. Given the years of pastoral experience, and my accumulating(!) life experience, in pastoral sessions I am tempted sometimes now to speak more than in the past. And when I catch myself in this situation I have to remember: Just listen.

The wisdom traditions of the ancient world are universal in commending the act and the importance of listening. These traditions caution us regarding too much speaking without enough listening. The Epistle of James fits into the genre of wisdom literature, carrying into the Christian era the tradition of Jewish wisdom, and in 1:19 we read: "...let everyone be quick to listen, slow to speak, slow to anger...." It was observed in the ancient world that we have two ears and one mouth for a reason. We typically should do about twice as much listening as speaking. Both the Hebrew Scriptures and the New Testament are replete with teaching on the importance of listening being the foundation for careful, thoughtful speech. In the Hebrew Scriptures, Proverbs contains numerous passages which speak to the importance of listening. Jesus addressed the subject in numerous settings. One particular verse from the Gospels is especially cautionary. In Matthew 12:36, Jesus says: "I tell you, on the day of judgment you will have to give an account for every careless word you utter...." Our Lord himself teaches that attentive listening is the foundation for careful, thoughtful, productive speech.

James's caution against too much speech and too much anger may seem counter-cultural to us. We live in an era of self-expression. One of the assumptions of our culture is that everyone can have their say. And of course, that is right. The rise of talk radio speaks to our cultural understanding that everyone should feel free to express his or her opinion. And with the advent of the internet and social media, now *anyone* can have their say on any subject. Now anyone can sit down at a keyboard and speak to the world.

Oftentimes in our culture there is much more speaking than listening. Frequently, I notice on both radio and television that everyone is talking at the same time. Of course, while this is happening no one is listening! Paul Tournier, one of the pioneers in modern pastoral counseling, urged caution regarding too much speaking and not enough listening, noting that when everyone is talking and no one is listening the result is "dialogues of the deaf."[1] And the English priest and spiritual writer Michael Mayne was fond of saying that when people are speaking but are not listening to each other what results is merely a disturbance of the air.

The Epistle of James is a wisdom book written for practical use among Christians. James did not write in a spiritual vacuum. The Epistle of James was written to be of practical use in the everyday lives of worshipers. And Christian congregations of his time would have been diverse. They would have been diverse theologically, with some congregants coming out of the Jewish tradition while others would have come into the church from a pagan background. Christian congregations included both men and women, and there would have been significant economic diversity in these assemblies, as Christian congregations accommodated much more socio-economic diversity than other groups in the culture at large. Every word of James is meant to be practical guidance for use in daily life, including congregational life. Craig Blomberg and Mariam Kamell in their commentary on 1:19 write: "Credible Christian relationships require careful attention to others' perspectives."[2] And in his commentary Kurt Richardson observes: "Wherever wisdom is the goal, hearing will be a first virtue."[3]

"Let everyone be quick to listen, slow to speak, slow to anger...." Of course, "be slow to speak" does not in the end mean "never speak." James certainly understood the power of words. After all, he wrote a book. No one, ancient or modern, writes a book for it to be ignored. People write books to add their voices to the conversation, to be heard. James knows that there is a time to take a stand against obvious injustice, obvious inequality. To be sure, people of faith must speak, and speak clearly. But James cautions us that speech should be carefully thought through. Speech should come from a foundation of attentive listening and thoughtful reflection. And, when we do speak, as people of faith must, we are always to think in terms of the impact that our speech will have. Is it constructive? Does it keep people engaged? Does what we say further meaningful conversation? James cautions us to be slow to speak, but *not* to be silent. In a summary comment on James's teaching on speech, Dan McCartney writes that to be slow to speak is: "...by no means an endorsement of a quiescent acceptance of the status quo."[4]

"Let everyone be quick to listen, slow to speak, slow to anger; for your anger does not produce God's righteousness." One size does not fit all, and one verse of Scripture cannot be expected to apply equally in all situations. When we study God's word it is the totality of the biblical narrative, its broad sweep, that we are to bear in mind, and thus one verse has to be interpreted in concert with other verses on the subject at hand.

With all of that said, let us please be clear—anger is a natural human emotion. Anger is a reality of life. And, ultimately, anger has to come to expression. Unexpressed anger tends to build over time and can lead to depression, even to rage. The Bible is clear regarding anger being a reality of life and is replete with passages that deal with anger, passages wherein people *are* angry and express their anger.

James cautions us to be *slow* to anger, "...for your anger does not produce God's righteousness." Of course we do get angry, and at times we should. The question is: How do we express anger? How do we deal with it? And what do we do with it that, ultimately, reflects God's love and will?

There is a place in the spiritual life for righteous indignation. Think of the prophets in the Hebrew Scriptures. Think of Jesus's cleansing of the Temple. Modern-day prophets at times rightly call us to righteous indignation. It is, however, incumbent upon us to be on guard concerning our righteous indignation vis-à-vis self-righteousness. Anger is a natural human emotion. It has to be acknowledged and expressed. But, in the end, people of faith are called primarily to be people of joy, and peace.

In my experience, the greatest contemporary exemplar of this balancing of righteous indignation and joy is Archbishop Desmond Tutu. While I do not know him personally, I have been in Archbishop Tutu's presence several times at conferences and worship services and have been careful to observe him over the years. Think about the overt prejudice, the outright hatred that Desmond Tutu has encountered in his lifetime. Think about the sheer volume of anger expressed toward him, and the countless threats that have been made against him. And yet, at every turn, Desmond Tutu has stood up for justice and equality, grounded in a theological vision of God's will for humanity that we live together in peace, with justice for all. Desmond Tutu has stood up for righteousness at every turn, sometimes at great personal risk, and yet he is *the* most joyful human being I have ever experienced. Having been in the same room with him on numerous occasions, I can say from personal experience that Archbishop Tutu radiates joy and love. Consider all that he has experienced in his lifetime and the righteous indignation that he rightly has expressed against prejudice and injustice, and yet he remains a loving, magnetic, joyful spirit.

James understands the place of anger, but he also understands that, ultimately, we gain the most perspective, the most wisdom—in the end our opinion is best informed—by listening. In his commentary on 1:19 Kent Hughes writes: "...an angry spirit is never a listening, teachable spirit."[5]

"Therefore rid yourselves of all sordidness and rank growth of wickedness, and welcome with meekness the implanted word that has the power to save your souls." The Greek for "rid yourselves" carries with it the connotation: remove your old clothing and put on new. The imagery here reminds us of early baptismal liturgies and reflects the tradition of the newly baptized donning fresh white clothing immediately following baptism. One would 'rid oneself' of old clothes prior to baptism and then put on new to represent having died to sin and being raised to newness of life.

"Welcome with meekness the implanted word that has the power to save your souls." The Greek for "meekness" carries with it the connotation of gentleness and, ultimately, a sense of humility. James 1:21 is cautionary to us all. Yes, we will be angered at times. And yes, there is a place for righteous indignation. But, in the end, we are meant to have a humble spirit and an abiding awareness that, ultimately, it is God who judges, and our primary stance in relationship to God, and each other, is one of humility.

In a summary comment on the meaning of 1:19-21, Ralph Martin writes that James's message to us, succinctly stated, is that in the name of Christ we are to: "...act responsively and responsibly."[6] Amen.

A TIME OF SOUL-SEARCHING

JAMES 1:22-25 • 2 JULY 2020

²²But be doers of the word, and not merely hearers who deceive themselves. ²³For if any are hearers of the word and not doers, they are like those who look at themselves in a mirror; ²⁴for they look at themselves and, on going away, immediately forget what they were like. ²⁵But those who look into the perfect law, the law of liberty, and persevere, being not hearers who forget but doers who act—they will be blessed in their doing.

In his commentary on the Epistle of James, Douglas Moo observes regarding 1:22 that it is: "...rightly the best-known verse in the letter."[1] Luke Timothy Johnson asserts that 1:22 reflects: "...the aim of all moral instruction."[2] And William Barclay interprets 1:22 to mean: "...what is heard in the holy place must be lived in the marketplace...."[3] Be *doers* of the word, and not merely hearers.... Wisdom traditions of the ancient world universally promulgate such teaching. The Hebrew Scriptures are replete with examples, particularly in the prophetic books.

James says in 1:21: "Therefore rid yourselves of all sordidness and rank growth of wickedness, and welcome with meekness the *implanted word* (emphasis mine) that has the power to save your souls." Here we are reminded of Jeremiah 31:33: "I will put my law within them, and I will write it on their hearts; and I will be their God, and they shall be my people." Jeremiah speaks on behalf of God that the law will be 'written' on our hearts. In 1:21 James refers to the "implanted word," which sets up verse 22: "But be doers of the word"—this *word* that is 'written on our hearts' as people of faith—the implanted word of God.

Jesus preaches and teaches the necessity of putting our faith into action. One of the best examples is Luke 11:27-28. Contextually, Jesus is in a crowd teaching, and amidst all of the concomitant frenzy and excitement surrounding Jesus, Luke tells us: "While he was saying this, a woman in the crowd raised her voice and said to him, 'Blessed is the womb that bore you and the breasts that nursed you!'" Not something we hear every day! This woman, in awe of Jesus and recognizing the holiness of the moment, cannot contain her joy. Yet even in the midst of such praise, Jesus's response is: "Blessed rather are those who hear the word of God and obey it!"

Paul is true to this line of teaching as well. One of the best examples is Romans 2:13: "For it is not the hearers of the law who are righteous in God's sight, but the doers of the law who will be justified."

The wisdom here is clear. Our actions are always to be guided by our understanding of truth. Our actions are to be congruent with our words. Sometimes this is easy. Oftentimes it is so easy to do the right thing that we really do not have to think about it. In such cases, doing what is right just comes naturally. But in other situations this is much more difficult. On the one hand, we may know exactly what we *should* do. And yet, it may be hard for us to follow through when we know that what we understand to be the truth differs from what the majority of those around us are thinking.

For most of us, our understanding of 'truth' evolves over time. My own reaction to recent events surrounding the deaths of Ahmaud Arbery and George Floyd is, in many ways, very different than what it would have been 30 years ago when I was first ordained. This personal example speaks to the possibility of evolution in our thinking. As time goes on we are meant to deepen our reflection, to broaden our perspective(s) on what we understand to be true.

In his commentary, Kurt Richardson says of 1:22 that it: "… captures James's burden for his hearers."[4] In other words, the essence of James's overarching message is contained within 1:22. Put succinctly, the thrust of James's wisdom is that we are to connect head to heart, word to action.

Independence Day is close at hand. Independence Day is considered by the Episcopal Church to be a Major Feast of the Christian year.[5] In *The Book of Common Prayer*, in the section "Other Major Feasts," Independence Day is listed right alongside Thanksgiving Day. And in the Prayer Book's calendar for the church year July 4 is clearly marked as a Major Christian Feast.[6] Independence Day has its own collect, and there is another collect in the Prayer Book, "For the Nation," which may be used in place of the collect for Independence Day.[7] Thus, not one but two prayers in *The Book of Common Prayer* speak specifically to the theological foundation and the spiritual dimension of Independence Day.

Independence Day, 2020, will have a different feel, a different texture. For one thing, we are in the midst of a global pandemic, the reality of which is coming closer and closer to home. Just last night I spoke at length with a survivor of COVID-19, and in great detail she spoke of just how difficult the struggle was and is for her, and of the heroic work of the doctors and nurses and other staff who cared for her and the other COVID patients. Given the global pandemic, and now the reality of social protests, this year's Independence Day will be a time of soul-searching for us as a nation. To miss this call to introspection would be to miss the moment.

The Independence Day upon us is destined to be different. The *moment* has changed. At the national level, what is happening may seem far removed from us. Even at a regional level we may be tempted to think: Well, that's in Chattanooga, or Nashville, or Atlanta. And yet here in Cleveland, Tennessee, we are grappling with the theological foundation and spiritual aspirations of our country and the abiding significance of our history in all of its ramifications.

Every workday for me is different. No two days are exactly alike. But most evenings I leave the church office between 7:00 and 7:15 pm. I try to get home for "Jeopardy" most nights. I get a good, healthy dose of humility each evening being reminded of just how much I don't know! By that time of evening, as I make my way up North Ocoee Street, protestors and counter-protestors have gathered again at the Civil War monument, typically in about equal numbers on opposite sides of the street. Every evening I drive right through the middle of two very different experiences and interpretations of American History.

This *is* a time of soul-searching for us. It is a time for all of us to remember the theological and spiritual underpinnings of this nation's aspirations for freedom, equality, and justice.

> **But be doers of the word, and not merely hearers who deceive themselves. For if any are hearers of the word and not doers, they are like those who look at themselves in a mirror; for they look at themselves and, on going away, immediately forget what they were like. But those who look into the perfect law, the law of liberty, and persevere, being not hearers who forget but doers who act—they will be blessed in their doing.**

We are about to celebrate our great national holiday. In doing so, I encourage us all to think of Independence Day not just in terms of a national holiday, but in terms of being a Major Feast of the Christian year. The time is right for us all to take to heart in a deeper way what it means to aspire to be: *"One Nation, under God, indivisible, with liberty and justice for all."* This year in particular, we are called to consider our Independence Day observance not just from the perspective of celebrating our national history and identity, but also in terms of our aspirations, and the hard, necessary work that lies before us. This year in particular, we are called to reflect on this challenging moment in our nation's history bearing in mind James's pastoral wisdom: Be *doers* of the word, and not merely hearers. Amen.

STICKS AND STONES

JAMES 1:26-27 • 9 JULY 2020

²⁶If any think they are religious, and do not bridle their tongues but deceive their hearts, their religion is worthless. ²⁷Religion that is pure and undefiled before God, the Father, is this: to care for orphans and widows in their distress, and to keep oneself unstained by the world.

Most of us will know the children's rhyme: "Sticks and stones may break my bones, but words will never hurt me." I have a memory of learning it in kindergarten. It is catchy and memorable. And, to be sure, the rhyme makes its point. We are to develop resilience in life. Indeed, it is imperative that we develop resilience. We must learn to stay calm when we are provoked and not retaliate in ways that we will regret. So, "Sticks and stones…" does make a point or it would not endure and be such a part of our culture.

"Sticks and stones may break my bones, but words will never hurt me." It is catchy and memorable and it makes a point, but in the end it is not true! In the end, it is simply not true. Words do hurt. While we were learning this rhyme as children we were also learning what it feels like to be embarrassed, humiliated, bullied. While we were learning this catchy rhyme and beginning to develop resilience we were simultaneously coming to terms with the reality that words do hurt.

Dan McCartney writes concerning 1:26-27: "...in James's summary of piety, a prime requirement of faithful behavior is control of the tongue."[1] McCartney introduces his comment with a key phrase: "In James's *summary* (emphasis mine) of piety...." An essential spiritual maxim, James is saying, is control of the tongue and recognition of the potential damage done through hurtful speech.

"If any think they are religious and do not bridle their tongues but deceive their hearts, their religion is worthless." Again the phrase from McCartney: "...James's summary of piety...." Scholars increasingly use the term "hinge" verse with regard to Scripture. In this hinge verse (1:26), James both reflects on what he has said up to this point in the letter and anticipates what lies ahead. In his commentary on 1:26 Kurt Richardson notes: "The tongue becomes the test case for true religion."[2] We all know the Gospel truism: "By their fruits you shall know them (Matthew 7:16, Douay-Rheims Bible)." James would include: By their speech you shall know them.

Words can build up, and they can tear down. Words can wound, and they can heal. In speaking so fervently about the importance of controlling our speech, James is, in the end, referring to discipline. We all have to learn discipline regarding both our speech and our actions. We must develop mental discipline to remember that our words can build up or they can tear down: our words can wound, as well as heal. In the spiritual life it is incumbent upon us to think, speak, and act in ways that are constructive rather than destructive.

I heard the advice years ago (the challenge is practicing it!) that in a situation in which we are tempted to speak in anger, tempted to speak out of frustration, tempted to retaliate, that it is a good idea to count to ten. Of course, in the heat of the moment the challenge is to *remember* to count to ten! It is one thing to agree in concept. The challenge lies in following through. But the teaching is valid: Count to ten before we say or do something that we might regret.

I cannot count how many times over the years I have been so very grateful that a letter I intended to send never saw a stamp. Far more often than not it is advisable to 'sleep on it' before we say or do something that in our gut we know is wrong. And now, in this era of social media, with so many platforms from which to speak, it is increasingly important to have thought through, to have reflected adequately on the question: Do I really want to hit Send?

In the leadup to Memorial Day I chose to read David McCullough's *1776*, a great book about that pivotal year in our nation's history. And in the leadup to Independence Day I chose to take on McCullough's biography of John Adams. Around these two major national holidays I chose a deep dive into the late eighteenth century (though I have to say that in between them I did slip in a book on C. S. Lewis). In that critical era in our nation's history it could take days, weeks even, for a letter to get from Boston to New York, or New York to Philadelphia. It could take days, if not weeks, for a letter to reach its destination. And thus when people wrote letters in those days every word counted, every word would have been thought through. Regarding transatlantic communication, in 1776 it could take three months at best for a letter to make it across the pond. Just imagine the care people would have taken to say exactly what they wanted to say for exactly the right reason(s). Every word mattered. In our time, words can be expressed instantly and easily (and thus thoughtlessly), and it is so important for us all to have the discipline to regulate, to be careful as to how we use our speech.

"Religion that is pure and undefiled before God, the Father, is this: to care for orphans and widows in their distress, and to keep oneself unstained by the world." There have been different times in my life when I have had this verse written out and taped to the back of a door, or to a wall, just to remind me of the importance of this basic, foundational teaching. Religion that is *pure* and undefiled before God, the Father, is this: to care actively, tangibly, for orphans and widows in their distress, and to keep oneself unstained by the world. In her commentary, Marie Isaacs writes of "orphans and widows" that for James they embody: "...Judaism's traditional ethic, in which widows and orphans epitomize all who are vulnerable due to no fault of their own. Their protection is a religious duty."[3] In James's world, as in the world of the Hebrew Scriptures, "orphans and widows" was a meaningful umbrella term, a catchphrase for the most vulnerable in society, those with the steepest hill to climb. "Orphans and widows" in the biblical era is an impactful rhetorical pairing referring to all those who are most susceptible to being disadvantaged through no fault of their own. The Hebrew Scriptures are replete with the call to care for "orphans and widows." And in the Gospels Jesus frequently reminds us to care for those who are most vulnerable. Further, at various points in the New Testament we see references to Paul taking up a collection for the poor in Jerusalem. The Hebrew Scriptures, Jesus, Paul—the Bible is consistent in the command to care for the most vulnerable in society.

In his comments on the term "orphans and widows," Luke Timothy Johnson refers to the "endemically impoverished."[4] We have all had to brush up lately on our understanding of the term "pandemic." A pandemic is wide-spread. Something that is "endemic" belongs to or is native to: "... a particular people or country."[5] A secondary definition of endemic is: "restricted or peculiar to a locality or region."[6] Malaria remains endemic to certain regions, to name just one example. Johnson, in referring to 1:27, reflects on orphans and widows representing the "endemically impoverished," and it is our duty as people of faith not just to pray for such persons, but to *see* them, and to respond in ways that meaningfully and impactfully reflect God's love and concern.

Kurt Richardson says of 1:27: "The poor are necessarily of chief concern to the church because they live under such travail. The unending tribulation of grinding poverty must move believers and their churches to assist the poor in every way, economically, legally, politically."[7] So here we have a contemporary reflection on and application of ancient Christian wisdom from the Epistle of James. Our necessary response to people who are endemically impoverished is to show forth all that we know and believe regarding God's love.

I came to be rector of St. Luke's in late May of 2003. The first day I was on the payroll I said to the office staff: "My only goal today is to learn the phone number. If by the end of the day I have learned the phone number, today will have been productive." Things picked up after that! The job took off after that first day. About three weeks into my tenure I contacted Matt Carlson, who then was director of our local chapter of Habitat for Humanity. Matt has become a friend in the years since, but in those early days I had not yet met him when I asked him to show me around Cleveland. He readily agreed, and I can remember saying to him on the appointed day as I got into his truck: "Show me the parts of Cleveland I haven't seen. Show me what no one else has shown me." And all these years later I can still remember Matt's exact words: "Pastor, within a mile and a half of this church, I can show you poverty that rivals anything in Appalachia." Those were his exact words. And over the next hour or so he proceeded to do just that. Within a mile and a half of this church building we *do* have poverty that rivals anything in Appalachia.

The theological truths that we believe most deeply about God's love—James calls us to live out these truths among those most in need. The call is just as important now as it was in the first century of the Christian era when James challenged his original hearers to religion that is meaningful to its adherents and transformative of society.

Faith at one level is inherently personal. Your faith is yours and my faith is mine, and at a certain level that is as it should be. But faith is also inherently communal, which we are learning more deeply during this time of social distancing. We just keep hearing: "I miss seeing people." Faith is personal, but faith is also communal. Of 1:27 Ralph Martin writes: "...however inward looking and individualistic personal trust must be, there is also a horizontal plane on which true faith operates."[8] Here Martin provides us with an insightful summary statement on James's message. There is a *vertical* dimension to faith, our 'personal relationship' with God. That said, James emphasizes that there is also the equally important *horizontal* plane on which we are to operate as people of faith.

"If any think they are religious, and do not bridle their tongues but deceive their hearts, their religion is worthless. Religion that is pure and undefiled before God, the Father, is this: to care for orphans and widows in their distress, and to keep oneself unstained by the world." "Unstained" is the most common translation of the Greek. Paul proclaims similarly in Romans 12:2: "Do not be *conformed* (emphasis mine) to this world, but be transformed by the renewing of your minds, so that you may discern what is the will of God—what is good and acceptable and perfect." Amen.

THE SIN OF DISCRIMINATION

JAMES 2:1-9 • 16 JULY 2020

¹My brothers and sisters, do you with your acts of favoritism really believe in our glorious Lord Jesus Christ? ²For if a person with gold rings and in fine clothes comes into your assembly, and if a poor person in dirty clothes also comes in, ³and if you take notice of the one wearing the fine clothes and say, "Have a seat here, please," while to the one who is poor you say, "Stand there," or, "Sit at my feet," ⁴have you not made distinctions among yourselves, and become judges with evil thoughts? ⁵Listen, my beloved brothers and sisters. Has not God chosen the poor in the world to be rich in faith and to be heirs of the kingdom that he has promised to those who love him? ⁶But you have dishonored the poor. Is it not the rich who oppress you? Is it not they who drag you into court? ⁷Is it not they who blaspheme the excellent name that was invoked over you? ⁸You do well if you really fulfill the royal law according to the scripture, "You shall love your neighbor as yourself." ⁹But if you show partiality, you commit sin and are convicted by the law as transgressors.

. . .

I n his commentary on 2:1-9, Kent Hughes writes: "James is preeminently a moral theologian."[1] We all have a sense of what "moral" means: "of or relating to principles of right and wrong in behavior."[2] James has written his epistle to encourage and help us to live lives in which our words are consistently matched by our actions. He writes succinctly and clearly in 1:22: "But be doers of the word, and not merely hearers."

James's writing style is crisp and clean, and he strings words together in such a way that his phrasing is memorable. Luke Timothy Johnson observes regarding 2:1-9: "James's reputation for vividness owes not a little to this passage."[3] The "vividness" of James's writing does indeed stick with us. Johnson also notes: "James sketches a situation in which readers fail to live by their convictions."[4] So again, James is primarily a moral theologian, encouraging us to behavior that matches the words, the belief structure of our faith.

Luke Timothy Johnson further observes: "James sketches human behavior that is virtually universal."[5] We human beings do tend to make distinctions immediately upon meeting someone based on the perceived differences between us rather than our underlying shared commonalities. We do tend to show favoritism. We are drawn to those who remind us of ourselves. It is nearly universal, and thus hard to overcome, the reality that we show favoritism, we make distinctions, and thus discriminate based on outward appearance.

James Adamson writes in his commentary on 2:1-9: "This passage exemplifies the enduring value of the Epistle of James as a caution to us against any complacent illusion of progress."[6] James cautions us not to assume, given what we profess in our faith, that our actions will automatically and in all cases follow suit. Adamson's comment offers an insightful summary statement not just of the passage, but of the entire epistle. James cautions us that we have to work at thinking in terms of equality and commonality rather than in terms of difference. We have to be intentional, says James, in seeing commonalities, rather than looking for distinctions. Kent Hughes is right: James *is* preeminently a moral theologian.

In 2:1 the term "favoritism" appears. The Greek for "favoritism" does not appear outside of the New Testament in extant Greek literature, its literal definition being: "to receive someone according to their face." A literal translation of the Greek might read: "Beware of receiving someone according to their face." Here is a straightforward warning against judging people based on externals. Most of us were taught as children: "You cannot judge a book by its cover." In 2:1 we have James's version: "Do not receive someone according to their face."

In 2:2, rather than "gold rings," a literal translation of the Greek is "gold fingers." The Greek connotes a person who has a gold ring on every finger. And regarding the wearing of "fine clothes," in the ancient world almost everyone wore homemade garments. It was only the very wealthy who could afford clothing that had been fashioned by someone else. Where I grew up we would call that "store-bought." In the biblical world, it was only the very rich who could afford store-bought clothing. Everyone else wore handmade garments. You, or someone in your house, or someone from the community would typically have fashioned the clothing you wore. The Greek in verse 2 is clearly painting a picture of great wealth: *obvious wealth* is really the key to its interpretation.

Regarding the term "poor person" in verse 2, in biblical Greek there are two words for "poor person." One connotes being destitute, utterly penniless. The other word for "poor person" has the connotation of not owning property, and thus conveys a 'softer' condition of poverty. The word James uses is the word for destitute. And the term "dirty clothes" in the New Revised Standard Version is a polite translation of the Greek, which can be translated literally as "filthy." This *destitute* person in verse 2 is wearing *filthy* clothes.

James has painted here a vivid portrait of a vivid contrast between an obviously wealthy person and an obviously destitute person. And then he notes in 2:4: "...have you not made distinctions among yourselves," have you not shown favoritism, "and become judges with evil thoughts?" When we instinctively are kind and inviting to a person wearing "gold rings and fine clothes" but are dismissive of someone who appears to be destitute, we have indeed made distinctions. The backdrop to this verse is in Leviticus 19, a chapter also important to Jesus in his own preaching and teaching. Leviticus 19:15 reads: "You shall not render an unjust judgment; you shall not be partial to the poor or defer to the great: with justice you shall judge your neighbor."

Regarding the backdrop to 2:6, Proverbs 14:31 reads: "Those who oppress the poor insult their Maker, but those who are kind to the needy honor him." And Proverbs 17:5 reads: "Those who mock the poor insult their Maker; those who are glad at calamity will not go unpunished." As is so often the case, the foundation for much of James's teaching lies squarely within Jewish wisdom literature.

And then in 2:8: "You shall love your neighbor as yourself." Again, Jesus drew heavily on Leviticus 19 in his own thinking, preaching, and teaching (cf. Mt 22:39; Mk 12:31; Lk 10:27). James refers to "You shall love your neighbor as yourself" as the "royal law"—a term unique to James. Scholars think that here James is offering an homage to Jesus. Jesus drew inspiration from Leviticus 19, and Jesus, being Messiah, or 'King,' James deems "You shall love your neighbor as yourself" as the "royal law."

We will remember 2020 for the rest of our lives. In the early days of this pandemic, those of us in this region were flooded with images from New York, Italy, China, Spain, etc. But over time the reality of the pandemic has come home to us. It has come to our region. It has come to our local area. And, make no mistake, it has come to this parish. The pandemic has now been visited upon the extended parish family of St. Luke's. During this time of pandemic we are powerfully reminded of the preciousness of life, the preciousness *and* the fragility of life. All thoughtful, reflective persons are being forced to confront the preciousness and fragility of the *gift* of life. We have been told over and over again by the finest medical experts that this virus does not discriminate. It can attack any of us. And so we are reminded periodically, and perhaps we should be reminded a little more often, that we are all in this together. This reminder accords with the theology that James highlights in 2:1-9: We are *all* in this *together* regarding the pandemic, and everything else.

The great English poet John Keats observed: "Nothing ever becomes real till it is experienced—Even a proverb is no proverb till your life has illustrated it."[7] This pandemic is getting more and more real to us. Now *we* are experiencing the reality of pandemic.

Those of us who come through 2020 will have seared into our memory forever the images surrounding the deaths of Ahmaud Arbery and George Floyd. In her commentary on 2:1-9, Sophie Laws offers her reflections on the passage under the section heading: "The Sin of Discrimination." And she translates 2:1: "My brothers, do not hold the faith in our Lord Jesus Christ, the glory, together with discrimination between people."[8] Here Laws provides a dynamic translation: "My brothers, do not hold the faith in our Lord Jesus Christ, *the glory* (emphasis mine), together with *discrimination* (emphasis mine) between people." And commenting on "favoritism" in 2:1, Dan McCartney writes: "The mandate in 2:1 is not a thesis needing to be proved; it is a general statement that the readers would have trouble disagreeing with, and it becomes the basis for an accusation and a call for behavioral change."[9] Amen.

I WILL, WITH GOD'S HELP

JAMES 2:14-17 • 23 JULY 2020

¹⁴**What good is it, my brothers and sisters, if you say you have faith but do not have works? Can faith save you? ¹⁵If a brother or sister is naked and lacks daily food, ¹⁶and one of you says to them, "Go in peace; keep warm and eat your fill," and yet you do not supply their bodily needs, what is the good of that? ¹⁷So faith by itself, if it has no works, is dead.**

When I was serving on the pastoral staff of St. Paul's, Chattanooga, one of our active parishioners was a man named Warren James. Warren had been Dean of Students at McCallie School for years. He had a very high profile in the church and in the local community and was a beloved figure in both. Warren had an exceptionally quick wit. He was a wonderful man.

Warren's wife was named Avis, and she had predeceased him by several years. After her death Warren lived alone for a number of years, and there came a point when he needed to have some surgery. It has been so long ago that I do not remember exactly what the surgery was, but I do remember the

"Thank You" note he sent to the church regarding our 'in-reach' to him once he was at home recovering from the surgery. While he was convalescing Warren wrote in gratitude to the parish: "Thanks to the prayers and good wishes of the people of St. Paul's, and some actual food from friends at Grace Church, I'm doing all right." The In-reach committee had gotten its wires crossed and had made an honest mistake. The left hand lost sight of the right hand, and while Warren got plenty of "Get Well" cards, he never received any actual food from St. Paul's! So, in the end, we were *all* grateful to the good people of Grace Church. "What good is it, my brothers and sisters, if you have faith but do not have works? Can faith save you?" The Greek for "works" can also be translated as "deeds." For James, faith leads to action. The foundational message of the Epistle of James is encouragement to *live* our faith, to have our actions mirror the words that we use to proclaim our faith. Our faith issues forth in deeds, concrete actions offered in the name of Christ. And our deeds, our actions, our "works," reflect our faith. The two, faith and works, are never in competition with each other, nor can one stand alone without the other—they feed each other, inform each other. Our faith is meant to lead us to deeds, and our deeds are to reflect, and are to be guided by and inspired by, our faith. The two, faith and works, continually inform and reflect each other. Faith and works are meant to fit each other like hand and glove.

The Hebrew Scriptures are replete with examples of encouragement to ethical behavior, and this theology is carried forward into the Christian era. In Luke 3:7-14 we have John the Baptist calling for faith to be reflected in action. Of course, Jesus was ever equating faith with deeds, actions of kindness and mercy. One of the great examples is Matthew 25:31-46, wherein Jesus says: "...for I was hungry and you gave me food, I was thirsty and you gave me something to drink, I was a stranger and you welcomed me, I was naked and you gave me clothing. I was sick and you took care of me, I was in prison and you visited me." Faith leads to action, and our actions reflect the faith that is in us.

Paul carries forward this understanding. He introduces Galatians 5:6 with: "For in Christ Jesus neither circumcision nor uncircumcision counts for anything...." This is not language that we typically would use in the twenty-first century! Of course, what Paul is referencing here is whether one is of Jewish heritage or from a Gentile background. Whether Jew or Gentile, Paul is saying, that in and of itself does not matter: "For in Christ Jesus neither circumcision nor uncircumcision counts for anything; the only thing that counts is faith working through love."

The Baptismal Covenant in the 1979 *Book of Common Prayer* has become foundational to our identity as Episcopalians. Every time we have a baptism in this church, and on other designated baptismal days, we say as part of the Baptismal Covenant: "Will you proclaim by word and example the Good News of God in Christ?"[1] By word *and* example. And the next question in the covenant is: "Will you seek and serve Christ in all persons, loving your neighbor as yourself?"[2] These are strong challenges, not just perfunctory spiritual rhetoric—real challenges meant to remind us that our faith and actions are to reflect, to mirror each other. Our answer to these challenges is: "I will, with God's help."[3] I *will* proclaim by word and example.... I *will* seek and serve Christ in all persons. I will, *with God's help*.

James 2:15: "If a brother or sister is naked and lacks daily food...." "Brother or sister" here is not an example of the New Revised Standard Version making the Greek text gender inclusive. "Sister" has not been added to suit our modern understanding of inclusivity. The word for sister is actually in the Greek text. The masculine form for 'sibling' is *adelphos*, the feminine form is *adelphē*, and both are in the Greek text: "If a brother *or sister* is naked and lacks daily food...." This is one of the few instances in all of the New Testament where the Greek for sister is actually in the text. What James is getting at here is the idea of family. We Christians are to be family to one another. We are to care for all family members equally.

In his commentary on 2:15, Solomon Andria writes: "There were certainly many poor people in the church to which James was writing."[4] And this certainly would have been true. There were no social safety nets in the world of the New Testament as we know them in our modern context. People without an adequate source of income, and lacking in family members to support them, could well have been very poor. We see numerous references to "the poor" throughout the Old and New Testaments that do not refer simply to people outside of the faith community. On this note Andria observes: "Fine sounding words would not feed them, nor would good wishes."[5] Thus James's pastoral encouragement: *See* your sisters and brothers who are in need. See them with love, and *respond* to their needs as best you can.

James 2:15-16: "If a brother or sister is naked and lacks daily food, and one of you says to them, 'Go in peace; keep warm and eat your fill,' and yet you do not supply their bodily needs, what is the good of that?" "Go in peace" here is the customary farewell of the biblical era. The Greek for "Go in peace" in the New Testament translates the Hebrew, *Shalom*, which speaks of God's peace: a sense of wellness, wholeness, that can only come from God. "Go in peace" in the New Testament is as 'religious' a farewell as one could muster. And yet, the question is, does the greeting, do the words, find their match in our actual care for others?

In a summary statement on the passage, Luke Timothy Johnson writes: "The necessary unity between attitude and action was the fundamental assumption of all ancient moral discourse."[6] And said unity is a hallmark of James's theology: the *necessary unity* between attitude and action. The two words go wonderfully well together: attitude and action. Johnson comments specifically regarding James's reference to "Go in peace": "It is not the form of the statement that is reprehensible, but its functioning as a religious cover for the failure to act."[7]

James is not scolding us here, he is instead encouraging us to remember that our words are always meant to find their match in our actions. The love of Christ is to inform consistently not only our attitude, but our actions as well.

Dan McCartney writes that James is advocating: "...actions that are as endemic to and characteristic of faith as heat is to fire or as breathing is to life...."[8] We are living in a time of global pandemic, and we have all been reminded recently of the actual meaning of "pandemic." "Endemic" is defined as: "belonging or native to a particular people or country...."[9] For James, actions of love and mercy are to be *endemic* to Christians. Such actions are simply constitutive of who we are as believers.

Then we encounter one of the most memorable verses in all of James, in all of the New Testament for that matter, 2:17: "So faith by itself, if it has no works, is dead." Here James articulates as clearly and concisely as is possible the essential relationship between faith and deeds—beliefs matched by actions.

It is difficult to imagine anyone who takes Christianity seriously who would deny James's message in 2:14-17. That said, the question is ever before us: Amidst the realities of everyday life, are our actions congruent with our beliefs? This time of pandemic is as important a time as ever for us to think in terms of our response to this foundational question. The pandemic forces us to reflect critically on our faith response in this particular moment when so much has changed for so many so quickly. In this time of lockdown, in its various phases, in this time of social distancing—how do we put James's teaching into action? How in this particular moment of uncertainty and anxiety can we serve as the hands and feet of Christ?

Some of us are working harder than ever during this time of

pandemic. People in certain vocations have had more asked of them in recent months than ever before. But many others of us have a little (or a lot!) more time on our hands than usual. This uncharted, unprecedented season, as challenging as it is, can be a kind of Sabbath time, a time to rethink and reimagine our response to Jesus's call to follow him. This moment can for many of us be 'found time' to take a step back from our normal routines and to think regarding going forward: What are my gifts for ministry in this new season? What are those things that I can do *now* to make a difference in people's lives? What are those things that Christ has enabled me to do, that I *can do* to show his love in this time of so much uncertainty and anxiety?

Clergy in the Diocese of East Tennessee had a Zoom call with our bishop early on in the pandemic. In concluding the call, our bishop, Brian Cole, said to us: "Do what you do best." In this new season, when in many ways we are having to re-invent how to be the church, Bishop Cole's pastoral advice to us in the end was: Do what you do best. In this unusual, unprecedented season, respond from the well of giftedness with which you have been blessed. "Do what you do best." Sound pastoral counsel now, and always.

This season is a time for us to recognize and to *claim* the gifts that we have been given, the gifts we have to offer in the name of Christ. James's pastoral wisdom in 2:17 rests upon the foundation of 1:22: "Be doers of the word, and not merely hearers." Amen.

IS IT LOVING?

JAMES 3:1-12 • 30 JULY 2020

¹Not many of you should become teachers, my brothers and sisters, for you know that we who teach will be judged with greater strictness. ²For all of us make many mistakes. Anyone who makes no mistakes in speaking is perfect, able to keep the whole body in check with a bridle. ³If we put bits into the mouths of horses to make them obey us, we guide their whole bodies. ⁴Or look at ships: though they are so large that it takes strong winds to drive them, yet they are guided by a very small rudder wherever the will of the pilot directs. ⁵So also the tongue is a small member, yet it boasts of great exploits. ⁶How great a forest is set ablaze by a small fire! And the tongue is a fire. The tongue is placed among our members as a world of iniquity; it stains the whole body, sets on fire the cycle of nature, and is itself set on fire by hell. ⁷For every species of beast and bird, of reptile and sea creature, can be tamed and has been tamed by the human species, ⁸but no one can tame the tongue—a restless evil, full of deadly poison. ⁹With it we bless the Lord and Father, and with it we curse those who are made in the likeness of God. ¹⁰From the same mouth come blessing and cursing. My

brothers and sisters, this ought not to be so. [11]Does a spring pour forth from the same opening both fresh and brackish water? [12]Can a fig tree, my brothers and sisters, yield olives, or a grapevine figs? No more can salt water yield fresh.

M any years ago a mentor of mine used to say to those of us in his charge that before we do or say anything, we should ask ourselves the question: Is it loving? Is what I am about to do or say loving? Of course, the challenge is to remember to ask the question! Amidst the routine of daily life, or in the heat of the moment—the challenge is to remember to ask the question: Is what I am doing, loving? Is this train of thought loving? Is what I am about to say, loving? Before any course of action, any speech, ask yourself the question: Is it loving?

A recurring theme in James is the importance of careful, thoughtful speech. James revisits the subject several times in his letter, including 3:1-12. In his comments on the passage Kent Hughes writes: "There are few sections of Scripture which are so graphically relentless in making a point."[1] James does stay after it, doesn't he? Hughes says further: "In addition, this is the most penetrating (and convicting) exposition of the tongue anywhere in literature, sacred or secular."[2] Here Hughes makes a strong claim: that we will not find any other treatments on careful speech that are any more detailed or instructive than 3:1-12.

On a recurring basis, James urges us to remember the importance of our speech being carefully thought through. In her commentary on 3:1-12, Pheme Perkins writes: "James challenges the casual attitude that many people take toward speech."[3] Of course, James wrote in the first century. If he were to come back from the dead, James would flip out at the way we use speech in our culture—at our carelessness with speech, our imprecision with words. Words come so easily, one might say cheaply, to us now via our many and varied platforms. James urges us to remember that words matter. How we use the precious gift of communication matters.

James was carrying forward Jesus's own teaching on careful speech. In Matthew 5:21-22 we read: "You have heard that it was said to those of ancient times, 'You shall not murder'; and 'whoever murders shall be liable to judgment.' But I say to you that if you are angry with a brother or sister, you will be liable to judgment; and if you insult a brother or sister, you will be liable to the council; and if you say, 'You fool', you will be liable to the hell of fire."

James carries on the teaching of Jesus, as Jesus carried forward the teachings of the Hebrew Scriptures on the importance of careful, thoughtful speech. In a summary comment on 3:1-12, Kent Hughes writes: "...whatever comes out of the mouth unfailingly reveals what is on the inside."[4] An insightful comment. When we say: "I didn't mean that," what we probably should say is: "I regret having said it." And "I didn't mean that," nearly always should be accompanied by: "I'm sorry for having said it." Whatever comes out of the mouth *unfailingly* reveals what is on the inside.

In 3:9 James is careful to use the pronoun "we." With the same mouth *we* bless and *we* curse. Earlier in the passage he writes in verse 2: "For all of us make many mistakes." James includes himself in his counsel. James faced the same temptations, the same challenges as we do in using speech carefully and wisely. With the same mouth *we* bless and *we* curse. James includes himself: "For all of us make many mistakes." James is as human as we are, and he goes to great lengths to impress upon us, himself included, the fact that the gift of speech is meant to be used to build up, not to tear down. In his commentary on 3:1-12, William Barclay writes: "It is one of life's hardest and plainest duties to see that the tongue does not contradict itself but speaks only such words as we would want God to hear."[5] Here is another way of framing the question: Is it loving? Would we want God to hear what we are saying? Is this train of thought or course of action in accord with Godly principles? Barclay chooses his words carefully here. It is one of life's hardest challenges to be careful with speech. And yet, he asserts, it is also one of our plainest duties. We know what we should do. The challenge is to be disciplined, to be mindful—always thoughtful about the impact of our speech and our actions.

One of the key passages in James is 1:26-27: "If any think they are religious, and do not bridle their tongues but deceive their hearts, their religion is worthless. Religion that is pure and undefiled before God, the Father, is this: to care for orphans and widows in their distress, and to keep oneself unstained by the world." In his commentary on 3:1-12, Luke Timothy Johnson, mindful of 1:26-27, offers: "James makes failure to control speech the very antithesis of authentic religion."[6] All of James's letter is interrelated and either anticipates what is to come, or reflects back on what has already been said. In 1:27 we have the signature verse: "Religion that is pure and undefiled before God...." Johnson, reflecting upon 1:26-27 *and* 3:1-12, asserts that failure to control speech is the very *antithesis* of authentic religion.

In studying 3:1-12 I am reminded of 1 John 4:20: "Those who say, 'I love God', and hate their brothers or sisters, are liars...." Here John echoes the teaching of James, who echoes the teaching of Jesus, who carries forward the teaching of the Hebrew Scriptures—our actions are to be consistent with our words.

James writes in 3:9: "With it [the tongue] we bless the Lord and Father, and with it we curse those who are made in the likeness of God." In his commentary on the verse Kurt Richardson writes: "One of the most important references to human nature in the New Testament is found here, for humans are in the *imago Dei*, created in the image and likeness of God."[7] Here James refers all the way back to Genesis 1:26-28, when in the creation story itself we learn that we are children of God, made in God's image and likeness. And so Richardson says further about verse 9: "To dishonor any human being in some way dishonors God."[8] When we curse someone, says James, we are cursing someone who has been made in the image and likeness of God. Thus his insistence, indeed his warning, on the importance of careful, thoughtful, measured speech.

In 3:10 James writes: "From the same mouth come blessing and cursing. My brothers and sisters, this ought not to be so." The Greek here is important to a proper interpretation in that it is the strongest possible wording of "...this ought not to be so." *The Common English Bible* offers a slightly different translation: "Blessing and cursing come from the same mouth. My brothers and sisters, it just shouldn't be this way!"

There are three basic tenets that I try to follow with regard to preaching. The first is: The best sermons are *about* the Gospel and *about* 10 minutes. The second is: Preach *to* yourself, not *of* yourself. And the third is: In preparing a sermon, have the Bible in one hand, and a newspaper in the other. The Epistle of James was written to real, flesh and blood Christians facing the same kinds of challenges we do. James wrote to Christians struggling to be faithful to their highest ideals. James was not written in a spiritual vacuum, and these meditations are not offered in a spiritual vacuum. There is nothing in the Epistle of James that is not directly relevant to our lives. This series of meditations is offered for this moment in time amidst a global pandemic and intense social stirring. They are not offered as an escape from reality, a few minutes of quiet and peace. Far from it. These meditations are meant to help us make sense of James so that we can apply his timeless wisdom and make sense of these challenging times, this difficult season in which we find ourselves.

The Epistle of James is as relevant for us now as it was for its original audience. These meditations are a deep dive into one of the most practical books in all of the Bible. Everything that James says we can take to heart, and be encouraged and guided as we try to live up to our highest ideals as followers of Christ. James goes to great lengths and takes great care in offering pastoral wisdom regarding how to speak and how to act because each person to whom we speak, each person on the receiving end of our action, is created in the image and likeness of God. Amen.

THE MARK OF TRUE WISDOM

JAMES 3:13-18 • 13 AUGUST 2020

¹³Who is wise and understanding among you? Show by your good life that your works are done with gentleness born of wisdom. ¹⁴But if you have bitter envy and selfish ambition in your hearts, do not be boastful and false to the truth. ¹⁵Such wisdom does not come down from above, but is earthly, unspiritual, devilish. ¹⁶For where there is envy and selfish ambition, there will also be disorder and wickedness of every kind. ¹⁷But the wisdom from above is first pure, then peaceable, gentle, willing to yield, full of mercy and good fruits, without a trace of partiality or hypocrisy. ¹⁸And a harvest of righteousness is sown in peace for those who make peace.

The first parish I served was St. Andrew's in Canton, North Carolina. The people of St. Andrew's were wonderful to their young, inexperienced pastor. I love those people to this day, and I remain in their debt. When I took up residence in Haywood County I became aware of a man named Clyde Kelly. He went by Kelly. Everyone called him Kelly. Kelly would drive in twenty minutes from the country every day and have breakfast at a local restaurant, and every day he would bring with him a stack of books and papers. He would read and write for the better part of the morning after having had breakfast. Others in the restaurant would make their way over to his table just to chat, or to seek out his wisdom. Eventually Kelly joined St. Andrew's and I became his pastor, and a beautiful friendship developed. But in the beginning I just knew him as Kelly, that brilliant, somewhat mysterious man who came into town every day for breakfast.

Before I got to know Kelly several people had remarked to me about him: "You know he's a retired Harvard professor." I had no real reason to doubt that, given his reputation as the wisest person in the county. But as it turns out, Kelly was a retired electrician! He had worked most of his career at the navy base in Key West, but he had also worked in D.C., and in the end had retired to a quiet life in Haywood County. Kelly had never even seen Harvard. He was, though, as wise a person as I have ever met.

In his maturity, John Adams, our second president, remembered having been a regular customer of a shoemaker in Boston many years earlier. This shoemaker, Adams recalled, always seemed happy. Adams remembered one particular encounter: "I had scarcely got out the door before he began to sing again like a nightingale."[1] This shoemaker was happily married, had a family, and enjoyed what he did for a living; he enjoyed interacting with his customers. Memories of the shoemaker's personal happiness and his apparent sense of fulfillment in his work prompted Adams to ponder from the perspective of his own maturity: Who was the greatest philosopher, Epictetus, or this shoemaker?[2]

It has been said about James that he is above all a moral theologian, and that is right. James is concerned at every step about right and wrong. It can also be said about James that he is ever a practical theologian. James carries forward into the Christian era the wisdom tradition that he inherited from the Hebrew Scriptures and from the intertestamental writings known as the Apocrypha. James is a wisdom text, but always accessible, practical, useful wisdom.

Peter H. Davids writes in his commentary on 3:13-18: "James states that not one's orthodoxy (right preaching) but one's orthopraxis (right living) is the mark of true wisdom."[3] A great insight. It is not only one's intellectual understanding of doctrine that makes for wisdom, but right living—having the wisdom to know *in the moment* what the right response is. It is not only right beliefs, but one's orthopraxis, right living, that is the mark of true wisdom.

In 3:13 we read: "Who is wise and understanding among you?" Here we find a key pairing of words: "wise" and "understanding." This pairing is unique to James in the New Testament but is frequent in the Hebrew Scriptures. "Wise" and "understanding" are paired together in Deuteronomy, in 1 Kings, in Job, and in Daniel. James asks in the Christian era: "Who is wise and understanding among you?" Then he continues: "Show by your good life that your works are done with gentleness born of wisdom." So here we get to the practical wisdom about which James is so passionate. Show by your good life, says James, by consistently doing the right thing, that you are gentle and wise.

While he was away at school and long before he would become our sixth president, John Quincy Adams received a letter (dated May 18, 1781) from his father which said: "You will ever remember that all the end of study is to make you a good man, and a useful citizen."[4] What a discerning understanding of practical wisdom. The end of all your studies, says father to son, is to make you a good man, and a useful citizen. The primary objective of education is to make us good, well-rounded people, and useful, civic-minded citizens.

James continues in 3:14: "But if you have bitter envy and

selfish ambition in your hearts, do not be boastful and false to the truth." Here we get to that chronic, ever present temptation —envy. C. S. Lewis observed regarding envy that the most persistent temptation throughout our lives, *the* most persistent temptation is a better seat at the table.

In 3:16 we read: "For where there is envy and selfish ambition, there will also be disorder and wickedness of every kind." In the Greek here "selfish ambition" more literally is translated as "party spirit," and thus James is getting at something specific to congregational life. He is warning against factions within a worshiping congregation, a constant temptation both in James's time and our own. In historical context, the more precise contextual meaning here may well be "party spirit." Do not be envious and do not show party spirit, as divisive factions have no place in congregational life.

Peter H. Davids observes regarding 3:16: "Rivalry and party spirit destroy the cohesiveness of the Christian community, which is built on unity and love."[5] It is always a challenge in congregational life to keep the focus on unity of the whole rather than allowing in a sense of party spirit. The cohesiveness of a Christian community is based on unity and love, not on who is 'right,' or who is more 'spiritual.'

Many of you will know the Jan Karon *Mitford* series, a runaway bestselling collection of books about a fictional church and a fictional priest and fictional people in a fictional town. Many years ago in a Christian Education class on the *Mitford* series I noted: "Anyone who thinks the *Mitford* books are fluff has never been the pastor of a small church!" Jan Karon has deep insight into congregational life, and *At Home in Mitford* includes the line: "A small parish is a fragile ecology."[6] That line has stuck with me for years now: A small parish is a fragile ecology. My only point, other than to agree, would be to say that this reality is not limited to small church life. All churches are fragile ecologies of new members and long-time members,

members who disagree with each other, in some cases passionately. Congregations are always a fragile mix of people, and it takes intentionality to work at cohesiveness and unity. We have to be intentional about congregational unity, whether in a small church or in a larger church setting.

James continues in 3:17: "But the wisdom from above is first pure, then peaceable, gentle, willing to yield, full of mercy and good fruits, without a trace of partiality or hypocrisy." Kurt Richardson notes regarding verse 17: "In this catalog virtually everything James had been saying...is summed up."[7] There *is* a lot of content in 3:17.

During hurricane season, when we see television coverage of a storm approaching our southern coast we almost always see palm trees in the background. And how are they faring in the wind? They are bending. They are flexible. They are yielding. But they seldom break. James is counseling us to be flexible. But his guidance does not in any way connote weakness or lack of principle. It is the wiser course to be flexible, to be willing to bend, to yield, when the moment dictates.

Peter H. Davids notes that James's understanding of wisdom encourages: "...a teachable spirit, a person who will gladly be corrected or learn a new truth."[8] A crucial aspect of practical wisdom is to be humble regarding all that we do now know. During the Civil War, Abraham Lincoln made a decision about troop movement and word got back to him through an aide that Secretary of War Edwin Stanton strongly objected to the decision, going so far as to call Lincoln a fool. And the story goes that Lincoln's response was: "If Stanton said I'm a fool, then I must be, for he is nearly always right. I'll see for myself."[9] And in due course Lincoln came to accept that he indeed had been wrong, and that Stanton was right. Even Abraham Lincoln, arguably our greatest president, had the wisdom to bend, to be flexible, to yield when the moment dictated.

In this time of social protests, I am frequently reminded of how my own convictions on race have changed over the years. And what I realize when I think about how my views have changed over time is that they keep changing, they keep evolving. This change, this evolution in my own thinking, comes largely from listening, from hearing different experiences and perspectives.

For there to be meaningful dialogue with those with whom we disagree, there has to be at least .1% of us that is willing to have our mind changed. Though we may be 99.9% convinced of our own position, for there to be real dialogue at least .1% of us has to be willing to change. This is the kind of gentleness, the willingness to yield, that James is advocating. In his commentary on 3:17 Kent Hughes perceptively observes: "A man or a woman is in a bad way when he or she is no longer persuadable."[10]

In 3:18 James writes: "And a harvest of righteousness is sown in peace for those who make peace." We reap what we sow (Galatians 6:7). In her commentary on verse 18 Marie Isaacs writes of the peaceable spirit that James is advocating: "...it is both the seed and its crop."[11] We gather in what we plant and cultivate. James counsels a peaceable, gentle spirit. The first line of the prayer attributed to St. Francis is: "Lord, make us instruments of your peace."[12]

In James's treatment of wisdom, everything he says on the subject is built on a foundation of humility, a healthy humility. I go back to John Adams's question in his maturity, looking back to his young adulthood and that shoemaker who was so happy and fulfilled in his vocation. Which was the greatest philosopher, asks our second president, himself one of the wisest thinkers this country, indeed the world, has ever known, Epictetus, or the shoemaker? The shoemaker was living a good, honest life. He enjoyed his life. He enjoyed serving other people. In her summary comment on James's understanding of wisdom, Sophie Laws writes: "Clearly James seeks to dissociate any claim to wisdom from a spirit of competition...."[13] Wisdom for James is not a matter of who is the smartest, or the most 'accomplished.' Wisdom for James, and for Jesus, is primarily about love, humility, responding in the moment in a way that shows compassion, fosters unity, and leads to peace. Herein lies real wisdom. Laws goes on to say regarding James's teaching: "Wisdom is understood in terms of moral virtue and practical goodness."[14] In the end, Christian wisdom is not so much about who is the smartest, but about how we treat other people.

Many years ago I came across an idea so profound in its simplicity that I can remember it to this day. This one line sums up much of what James, and, for that matter, Jesus, are trying to teach us: Practice having no ego, and you will be free. Amen.

AN INVITATION TO HEALING

JAMES 4:7-10 • 20 AUGUST 2020

⁷**Submit yourselves therefore to God. Resist the devil, and he will flee from you. ⁸Draw near to God, and he will draw near to you. Cleanse your hands, you sinners, and purify your hearts, you double-minded. ⁹Lament and mourn and weep. Let your laughter be turned into mourning and your joy into dejection. ¹⁰Humble yourselves before the Lord, and he will exalt you.**

Douglas Moo writes of this passage: "Here, if anywhere, we find the heart of James's letter."[1] A sound observation. One can make the case that everything James has said up until now has been building toward 4:7-10. David Nystrom writes about these verses: "The call of James is to a reorientation to God and his purposes in our world, purposes that touch on the social, cultural, and economic juggernauts with which human beings must reckon."[2] Everything James writes is meant to be of practical use in everyday life, and thus Nystrom is wise to note that, in the end, everything James has to say is relevant to social, cultural, and economic issues both ancient and contemporary. Everything that James espouses in this letter is meant to help real people in real circumstances make sense of everyday life from the point of view of faith.

In a real sense, in 4:7-10 we are dealing with the heart of the epistle. The argument in verses 7-10 follows on from the preceding six verses, which deal with envy and its fallout. One of James's recurring themes is that people of faith, like anyone else, can tend to become so friendly with the world that we lose focus on God's principles. Periodically James deals with what he calls "double-mindedness," a term unique to James in the New Testament. We first encounter the term in 1:8. For James, envy can also manifest as arrogance. Thus we read in 4:6: "But he gives all the more grace; therefore it says, 'God opposes the proud, but gives grace to the humble.'" Here James is quoting Proverbs 3:34: "Toward the scorners he is scornful, but to the humble he shows favor."

James uses language marvelously and memorably in 4:7-10. In 4:7-8 we read: "Submit yourselves therefore to God. Resist the devil, and he will flee from you. Draw near to God, and he will draw near to you. Cleanse your hands, you sinners, and purify your hearts, you double-minded." Kent Hughes notes regarding this passage: "This is a tidy unit, consisting of a series of terse commands...."[3] Ralph Martin observes that here James uses: "...a staccato burst of rapid commands...."[4] Indeed, the "staccato burst of rapid commands" here calls to mind the rhythm of a jackhammer in use.

It is noteworthy that James uses the term "you sinners" in 4:8. Up until now, everywhere else in the letter he has addressed his readers as: "brothers and sisters." There is a definite change of tone in verse 8: "...you sinners...." James wants to get his readers' attention! That said, it is crucial for us to remember that his change in tone here is more than balanced by the fact that everywhere else in the letter so far he has addressed his audience lovingly and pastorally as: "my brothers and sisters."

James is certainly concerned with nurturing a pastoral relationship with his readers. Still, there are moments that require a different tone, a different attitude, in order to get the audience's attention in driving home a point.

In verse 8 we read: "Cleanse your hands, you sinners, and purify your hearts...." James is referring here to Jewish cleansing rituals, rites of purification. All Jews would have known about the purity laws and the rites that accompanied them. And so, "Cleanse your hands..." here has to do with *external* reality, whereas "...purify your hearts..." deals with our *internal* disposition. "Cleanse your hands..." has to do with our external actions and "...purify your hearts..." reminds us that our external actions are dependent upon our internal disposition. Douglas Moo observes regarding our outward rituals and our inward attitude that we have to be concerned with "...deed and disposition."[5] How we respond outwardly depends upon our 'heart,' our internal spiritual disposition.

Early on in the epistle, James says in 1:22: "But be doers of the word, and not merely hearers...." In 4:8 he revisits the theme that our actions in the world, our everyday practical interactions with people, are meant to be guided by our spiritual principles. Ralph Martin notes that here: "...James connects inward disposition with outward social concern...."[6] It can truly be said of this letter that *everything* in it is meant to be of practical use. What we know to be right, theologically and spiritually, is meant to show forth in the real world in our interactions with other people.

In 4:9 we read: "Lament and mourn and weep. Let your laughter be turned into mourning and your joy to dejection." Here James addresses the subject of repentance, the need for all people of faith to review continually our ongoing need of repentance, a course correction. In real time, James was particularly concerned with the issue of "double-mindedness." But it is important to recognize that, though James takes a different tone for the moment in 4:7-10, he will end the section on an upbeat, positive note, that of grace. Different moments require different tones. But, in the end, James always leads his readers toward grace—God's compassionate and merciful forgiveness.

In reflecting on 4:7-10 Kent Hughes observes: "None of us came to Christ unbowed."[7] We all have sinned. We all have our times when we veer from the path we know we are meant to tread. It is true—none of us comes to Christ unbowed. The ardor of James's call to repentance here is not meant to be guilt-producing without hope of refreshment. The call to repentance is, instead, an invitation to healing and restoration—to grace. Here we are reminded of Isaiah's invitation to abundant life in 55:1: "Ho, everyone who thirsts, come to the waters...."

In his commentary on 4:7-10, Ralph Martin writes: "These negative attitudes should not be construed as though the preacher was a kill-joy."[8] Indeed, James is not a kill-joy. Martin continues: "But this reaction is for purposes of restoration."[9] James's call to repentance, his call to soul-searching is, in the end, an invitation to healing. And thus, ultimately, the call to repentance is an invitation to joy. Of James's call for repentance William Barclay observes that this represents: "...by no means the end of the Christian life."[10] Barclay continues: "The terrible sorrow of the realization of sin moves on to the thrilling joy of sins forgiven."[11] Acknowledging our need of God's forgiveness can be the first step toward receiving the "thrilling joy" of sins forgiven, the 'fresh air' of a new beginning.

In thinking about this meditation, I could not get out of my mind the speech that Jim Valvano gave during the 1993 ESPY Awards. Valvano was there to receive the Arthur Ashe Courage and Humanitarian Award. If you have not heard it lately, or if you have never heard this stirring speech from Jim Valvano, you can find this 10-minute speech on the internet. It would be good for all of us to revisit Valvano's inspiring remarks on a regular basis. Jim Valvano, the former North Carolina State

Men's Head Basketball Coach and popular television analyst, was dying of cancer when he was named the Arthur Ashe Award recipient. There is a point in his acceptance speech when Valvano, as a dying man, says that we should do three things every day. First, we should be sure to *laugh* every day. He then goes on to say that we should *think* every day. We should carve out time for reflective, substantive thought every day. And then the third thing we should do every day is *have our emotions moved to tears*, either tears of sorrow, or tears of joy. Something, or someone we care about should move our emotions to tears every day. We should laugh, think, and have our emotions moved to tears every day. Valvano then adds: "That's a full day. That's a heck of a day."

Every day we should laugh, think, and have our emotions moved to tears. Every day we are meant to experience a range of emotions. James certainly offers us different tones, a range of different emotions. At the heart of James's message, his impassioned pastoral appeal to readers, is his acknowledgment that, at an intellectual level, his readers know their religious obligations. His audience has at their disposal an adequate framework of faith. They have all the tools they need to live a spiritually fulfilling life. But James knows that the trick, the challenge, is to put all of that knowledge into action. Taken as a whole, the Epistle of James is an impassioned call to faith that leads to action: a faith wherein the internal and external dimensions of spirituality are in sync.

In 4:10 we read: "Humble yourselves before the Lord, and he will exalt you." Here James reclaims a more positive tone. A key plank in James's presentation of the Gospel is humility, a healthy, life-giving, life-guiding humility. On this note Rea McDonnell observes: "Humility is not passivity, but receptivity. It is certainly not groveling before God or others; it is simply accepting truth, learning from every situation, growing in simplicity, and in wisdom."[12] Humility here for James in no way suggests low self-regard. We are children of God, made in God's image and likeness. James's call to humility is rather a call to remember the foundation of faith that we have been given, and to put that faith into action in gratitude to God, and in the service of others. Three times, in three different places and situations, in Mt 23:12; Lk 14:11; and Lk 18:14, Jesus proclaims: "For all who exalt themselves will be humbled, and those who humble themselves will be exalted."

"Humble yourselves before the Lord, and he will exalt you." The Greek here in 4:10 for "exalt" carries with it a connotation of being lifted up. James ends this pivotal section of his epistle on a positive, encouraging note. The call to repentance is a call to healing and, ultimately, the promise of spiritual joy. Humble yourself, and God will lift you up.

The English priest and spiritual writer Michael Mayne frequently offered in his sermons that God's judgment is always more than matched by his mercy. Pastoral wisdom to remember, and to be guided by: God's judgment is *always* more than matched by his mercy. James's plea to his hearers to humble themselves is a plea to them to receive, to welcome, God's mercy. And then, of course, we are to share that mercy with others through our actions grounded in and guided by our faith.

William Barclay observes regarding 4:7-10: "The humility for which James pleads is not a cringing subservience."[13] And indeed, that *is not* what humility means here. What James is urging us to is a humility that takes the place of arrogance. In their commentary, Craig Blomberg and Mariam Kamell observe regarding James and his call for humility that James's message is the reminder: "...everything one is and has stems from God's lavish grace."[13] Amen.

ALL THAT WE REALLY HAVE IS NOW

JAMES 4:11-17 • 27 AUGUST 2020

[11]Do not speak evil against one another, brothers and sisters. Whoever speaks evil against another or judges another, speaks evil against the law and judges the law; but if you judge the law, you are not a doer of the law but a judge. [12]There is one lawgiver and judge who is able to save and to destroy. So who, then, are you to judge your neighbor? [13]Come now, you who say, "Today or tomorrow we will go to such and such a town and spend a year there, doing business and making money." [14]Yet you do not even know what tomorrow will bring. What is your life? For you are a mist that appears for a little while and then vanishes. [15]Instead you ought to say, "If the Lord wishes, we will live and do this or that." [16]As it is, you boast in your arrogance; all such boasting is evil. [17]Anyone, then, who knows the right thing to do and fails to do it, commits sin.

There are several recurring themes in the Epistle of James. James clearly understood the importance of repetition. As a sports fan, I am reminded of the time in basketball history when Michael Jordan and Larry Bird were each in their prime. It was understood around the league that, in the lead up to game-time, the first player out of the locker room for their respective teams for warm-ups would be Michael Jordan or Larry Bird. The finest players of their era, the players with the most prestige, the most fame—still, Michael Jordan and Larry Bird were first out of the locker room in preparation for game-time. They understood the importance of repetition. It was what had gotten them there and kept them at the top of their game. James understands the importance of repetition in his framing of the fundamentals of a life of faith.

I have never been great at math. I do not enjoy thinking about numbers. I *can* function mathematically, I can do *basic* math, but I have never enjoyed it. I still don't care what "x" is. I did not care in junior high or high school, and I do not care now! But I am glad that there are those who do. It is comforting to me that C. S. Lewis did not like math either. Just think for a moment regarding the stature, the legacy of C. S. Lewis. Lewis never passed the math exam required for admission to Oxford, and if he had not been a veteran of World War I, he would have been denied admission because of his deficiencies in math. Those of us who really do not care for math can take comfort in the fact that for some of us it is just not our thing. I say all of that to say this: All these years later, I can still remember my basic multiplication tables that I learned in elementary school. Why? Because of repetition.

Liturgy embodies the importance of repetition. There is a rhythm to Anglican liturgy, for instance. There is a prescribed order to the components of liturgical worship. We follow the same basic order of service every week. What differs is the moment, the Scripture lessons assigned, the prayers for the occasion, and, of course, the sermon. But the basic framework is set and is employed day after day, week after week. Liturgy is built on repetition.

There are recurring themes in James. As an author and teacher he understands the importance of hitting his main themes more than once, albeit from a slightly different angle and with a slightly different emphasis each time. Repetition is how we learn, it is how we remember.

Speech is a recurring theme in James. In 4:11 we read: "Do not speak evil against one another, brothers and sisters. Whoever speaks evil against another or judges another, speaks evil against the law and judges the law; but if you judge the law, you are not a doer of the law but a judge." Here, once again but from a different angle, with a nuanced emphasis, James reminds us of the importance of controlling our speech and the importance of using our speech for good. Certainly this teaching on careful speech is applicable to life in general, but in verse 11 James is specifically addressing the Christian community. Of all places, the church should be *the* place where we recognize the importance of careful, constructive speech.

In his commentary on 4:11, N. T. Wright observes: "[James] seems to have in mind the kind of slander or gossip which eats its way like a cancer in a Christian fellowship and requires urgent treatment if it is not to prove fatal."[1] Fortunately, not every church is consumed with gossip. But it is a constant temptation and something we always have to be on guard against. Dan McCartney notes of uncontrolled speech in the church: "It appears to be a problem *endemic* to the Christian community."[2] A significant charge. While I do not disagree with McCartney, I would widen the point to say that it is endemic to the *human community*, to any group—this temptation to use speech negatively.

I was not born to the Episcopal priesthood and had many different jobs along the way before I settled into the life of the pastorate. In every work environment and every social network I have ever been a part of there always was gossip—people 'talked.' Unhelpful speech happens everywhere. It is endemic to humanity.

Kent Hughes writes regarding 4:11: "...the command here forbids *any speech* (whether it is true or false) which runs down another person."[3] A particularly insightful comment. James cautions us against evil speech, slander broadly defined—'loose talk.' And in so doing he cautions us regarding judging other people, even though in some cases what is being said may actually be true. Still, if our line of speech is not leading somewhere constructive, we are better off not going there. What James is addressing here is not just falsehoods, or even half-truths. He is cautioning us against any speech that, in the end, is not loving, is not constructive—speech that does not add anything positive to the conversation.

Hughes also mentions regarding 4:11 the danger of what he calls "corrosive speech."[4] This refers to patterns of speech that, in the end, simply are not productive. We all fall into habits, patterns of speech that are not constructive. Negativity has a way of feeding on itself and perpetuating itself. On more than one occasion, I have had the realization: "I don't even want to hear this anymore, let alone verbalize it to others." Corrosive speech is as damaging to the speaker as it is to its audience. James is working to lift us out of negative habits into more positive use of God's gift of speech.

In 1 Peter 4:8 we read: "Above all, maintain constant love for one another, for love covers a multitude of sins." In commenting on 4:11, Peter Davids writes, with 1 Peter 4:8 also in mind: "'Love covers a multitude of sins.' It does not broadcast sins, so Christians must not speak negatively about others."[5] There are certain things we just do not need to talk about. Sometimes the best use of our gift of speech is silence. Davids goes on to observe: "To criticize another is neither love nor is it the way one wishes to be treated oneself."[6]

Then 4:12: "There is one lawgiver and judge who is able to

save and to destroy. So who, then, are you to judge your neighbor?" This is one of the prime examples in all of Scripture of cautioning against judgmentalism. Another of the recurring themes in James is humility. Careful speech and a proper sense of humility are recurring themes in James and go hand-in-hand. In 4:12 the call to humility is framed in terms of anti-judgmentalism. In his commentary on verse 12, Luke Timothy Johnson writes that what James is offering here is a condemnation of judgmentalism that: "...arrogantly assumes a superiority over the other."[7] We cannot be humble if we are thinking of ourselves as being superior to others. Kurt Richardson adds: "Only God, who knows the secrets of the heart, only God can judge the heart."[8] And Dan McCartney reminds: "...no individual in the community is in any position to judge the spiritual condition of another."[9]

Clearly, there are unacceptable behaviors. Certain actions are simply wrong. Here we are reminded that James is preeminently a moral theologian. James's teaching on proper speech does not connote a life of quietism, a life wherein we never speak up. Of course not. Some actions are inherently wrong, inherently hurtful or harmful. And such actions must be challenged. What we *are* called to in James is a general attitude of humility that enables us to refrain from constantly having a negative or critical perspective towards others. To this end, Kent Hughes writes of 4:12: "What the scriptures forbid is *judgmentalism*, a critical and censorious spirit that judges everyone and everything...."[10] To be sure, there are specific behaviors which are unacceptable, and against which Christians must take a stand. But a general attitude where we are always looking to be critical, or thinking of ourselves as being better than others, is what James is cautioning us against. Have the humility, James is teaching, to understand that we all are on equal footing in the eyes of God. Encouragingly, Hughes adds regarding 4:11-12: "We have the life of Christ in us."[11] And: "It is possible to lead lives which heal instead of bite, which sustain instead of take."[12]

A couple of weeks ago I was talking with a priest friend about this series of meditations and he said: "I like James, but he can get a little preachy at times." True, but then again, James *is* a preacher! And in the end James's preaching is meant to encourage us. James has our best interests at heart. He is on our side. Thus Hughes's observation is insightful. We *can* do better. We have *the life of Christ* in us. The spirit of Christ calls us to healthy behaviors, to a hopeful, positive mindset—a disposition to love and be patient with others rather than being constantly irritated or critical, and thus, judgmental.

In 4:13-14 we read: "Come now, you who say, 'Today or tomorrow we will go to such and such a town and spend a year there, doing business and making money.' Yet you do not even know what tomorrow will bring. What is your life? For you are a mist that appears for a little while and then vanishes." In her commentary on this passage, Sophie Laws writes: "The theme is a universal one...."[13] Ancient wisdom texts are filled with this understanding: none of us knows what tomorrow may bring. In the Hebrew Scriptures, Job contains numerous such references. We must not be presumptuous regarding the future. The Psalms also contain numerous references to the understanding that we should focus on today, the moment that is now, rather than presumptuously assuming a future that is, in reality, only an assumption.

When we were celebrating the New Year just a few months ago, though in some ways it seems like a lifetime, none of us could have imagined where we are today. The pandemic, and now this time of social protests are powerful reminders that we are to be cautious about assuming the future. None of us *knows* beyond this moment. And so, it is this moment that matters most. What can we control today? What can we do today? James would remind us that every day is, ultimately, a gift. James joins in the universal chorus of ancient wisdom: Do not be presumptuous about the future. Live in the moment. Of course, we are to make prudent plans, prudent provisions for the future. But in the end all that we really have is now.

James 4:17 reads: "Anyone, then, who knows the right thing to do and fails to do it, commits sin." Throughout the epistle James is adamant that our faith and our actions are meant to be congruent. And so we have here in verse 17: "Anyone, then, who knows the right thing to do [from a faith perspective] and fails to do it [i.e., concretely in daily life], commits sin." We may be tempted to regard sins of *omission* as being relatively benign compared to sins of *commission*. But James challenges us here. He presses us on the tacit, perhaps even unconscious, assumption that sins of omission are not as significant as sins of commission.

James Adamson notes in his commentary on 4:17: "James concludes this chapter...with a pointed sententious maxim: 'Not to do what you know to be right is sin.' The phrase *does not do it*, does *not* merely signify a sin of omission; the omission of 'good' is necessarily a doing of 'evil.'"[14]

A careful, receptive reading of James pushes us out of our comfort zones. To know the right thing to do requires us to do the right thing. Amen.

CARELESS LUXURY

JAMES 5:1-6 • 3 SEPTEMBER 2020

¹Come now, you rich people, weep and wail for the miseries that are coming to you. ²Your riches have rotted, and your clothes are moth-eaten. ³Your gold and silver have rusted, and their rust will be evidence against you, and it will eat your flesh like fire. You have laid up treasure for the last days. ⁴Listen! The wages of the laborers who mowed your fields, which you kept back by fraud, cry out, and the cries of the harvesters have reached the ears of the Lord of hosts. ⁵You have lived on the earth in luxury and in pleasure; you have fattened your hearts in a day of slaughter. ⁶You have condemned and murdered the righteous one, who does not resist you.

At different stages of his letter, James takes different tones. This is a requirement of leadership. It is important to remember that, far more often than not, James starts a section with "brothers and sisters," expressing solidarity with his readers, even kinship. But there are those moments when James takes a different tone, such as in 5:1: "Come now, you rich people, weep and wail for the miseries that are coming to you."

Commenting on 5:1, Kent Hughes writes: "James' attack in the opening paragraph of chapter 5 can only be described as 'seething.'"[1] Scholars debate as to whom these comments are addressed. The majority view is that these "rich people" are non-congregants. Instead, they are wealthy, powerful land owners who are systematically taking advantage of day laborers, lining their own pockets with what more justly would be paid out to the workers.

N. T. Wright comments on 5:1: "This is one of the sharpest warnings against careless luxury anywhere in the Bible."[2] "Careless luxury" is a term that Wright has chosen carefully. Financial success as such is not under attack here, but what Wright calls "careless luxury." What *is* under attack here is economic prosperity that is not shared justly. And so, Luke Timothy Johnson writes commenting on 5:1: "The reader is startled by the energy and force of the opening: the rich are to 'weep and wail' over the miseries that are coming upon them."[3] In the New Testament we do not see the Greek word for "wail" other than here, but the Hebrew for "wail" runs all through the prophetic writings of the Old Testament. To "weep and wail" is to anticipate judgment, and thus Johnson's note that the reader is "startled" here by James's usage. We have gotten "brothers and sisters" a lot in this letter, but the tone changes in 5:1-6. Johnson also notes: "James does not condemn wealth as such but the greed and injustice involved in creating it."[4] *Injustice* is the key word here. It is not the money itself, but the careless lack of regard for the powerless, who have played such a large part in generating the income, that is judged here.

Elsewhere in the New Testament, Joseph of Arimathea is a person of wealth who is commended.[5] Also, Zacchaeus is a person of means who is commended for his change of heart.[6]

And Lydia is clearly a successful businesswoman.[7] In 1 Timothy 6:10 we read: "For the love of money is a root of all kinds of evil, and in their eagerness to be rich some have wandered away from the faith and pierced themselves with many pains." A classic statement from Paul framing the issue of faithful stewardship. It is the *love* of money that is the root of evil, and the lure of wealth and its subsequent hoarding can be a nearly irresistible temptation away from a life of humble, generous faith. It is the craving for more than we need that puts us in spiritual jeopardy. It is *careless luxury*, a heartless lack of concern for the poor, that is being judged in this passage.

In a summary comment on 5:1-6, Luke Timothy Johnson writes: "James devotes to it some of his most vivid language, adopting once again the rhythms of the great social prophets of Israel, who had also railed against the oppressive rich."[8]

In 5:2-3 we read: "Your riches have rotted, and your clothes are moth-eaten. Your gold and silver have rusted, and their rust will be evidence against you...." The Old Testament prophets referred to riches "rusting." And two millennia on from the writing of James we yet know the meaning of "moth-eaten" clothes—they have not been worn. What is being pictured here are people who have so much that they do not even use what they have, and the 'extra' could be painlessly redistributed to the poor. James employs powerfully clear imagery here: "moth-eaten" clothes are so far back in the closet that they are not being used. They may even have been forgotten. Clearly what James is against here is selfishness, a callous disregard for the poor. He warns against holding on to more than we need instead of cultivating a spirit of generosity and a ready willingness to share. It is selfishness that is being challenged here, not abundance in and of itself.

The tradition regarding James is that he is Jesus's brother. Jesus says in Matthew 6:19: "Do not store up for yourselves treasures on earth, where moth and rust consume and where thieves break in and steal...." In 5:1-6 James's teaching is directly in line with that of Jesus. Jesus continues in Matthew 6:20-21: "...but store up for yourselves treasures in heaven, where neither moth nor rust consumes and where thieves do not break in and steal. For where your treasure is, there your heart will be also." Whatever the historical connection between the author of the Epistle of James and Jesus himself, their teaching here could not possibly be more closely aligned.

James 5:4 deals with overt mistreatment of day laborers. In a number of Jesus's parables, workers and laborers are involved in the stories, and, inevitably, the point is for those with power to be fair to those without. The teaching in 5:4 is built on the theology of Leviticus 19, clearly an important backdrop for our author. In Leviticus 19:13 we read: "You shall not defraud your neighbor; you shall not steal; and you shall not keep for yourself the wages of a laborer until morning." The teaching here is clear: Do not say to those who have worked for you all day, "I will pay you tomorrow." In a society which lacked enforceable labor regulations, the landowner could get away with unfair practices. And thus James's teaching in our passage is fully in line with the ethical standards set forth in the Hebrew Scriptures. James continues in verse 4: "Listen! The wages of the laborers who mowed your fields, which you kept back by fraud, cry out, and the cries of the harvesters have reached the ears of the Lord of hosts." Here again James carries forward Jesus's concern for the poor. And Jesus's concern was squarely grounded in the Hebrew Scriptures, with their long tradition of advocacy of compassion and justice for the poor.

Scholars have observed that in the economy of first-century Palestine, it could be less expensive to pay day laborers than to maintain slaves: wages for day laborers being so low. Again, there was no regulation of labor laws like we experience in our culture, and, in comparison with our society, there were no social safety nets, and thus the poor were even more vulnerable then than now. On this note Kent Hughes writes: "This sin [the systematic mistreatment of poor workers] is not confined to a Dickens novel."[9] A great turn of phrase. Unfair labor practices are not confined to the biblical era, *nor* to a Dickens novel. The issue of fairness for people who work, and yet struggle to have life's basic necessities, is as real today as ever.

James 5:6: "You have condemned and murdered the righteous one, who does not resist you." "Righteous one" here is collective, and James's language is particularly vivid: 'You have *condemned* and *murdered* those so economically and socially powerless that they have no means to resist.' What James is crusading against here is a collective carelessness in regard to those so economically disadvantaged that they are forced to live hand to mouth. In their commentary on verse 6, Craig Blomberg and Mariam Kamell assert, citing Ecclesiasticus 34:21-24: " In the Jewish world, to deprive a person of their support was the same as murdering them."[10] To deny people their earned wages is, in effect, to deny them food, and to place their housing in jeopardy, and thus their ability to care for themselves and their families. The domino effect of careless, callous, indeed predatory exploitation of the poor is to put their very lives in jeopardy. Squarely in line with Jewish theology, James writes: "You have *condemned* (emphasis mine) and *murdered* (emphasis mine) the righteous one [the poor], who does not resist you." A 'careless luxury' can actually lead to the deaths of souls precious in the eyes of God.

Again Luke Timothy Johnson's summary statement on 5:1-6: "James devotes to this passage some of his most vivid language, adopting once again the rhythms of the great social prophets of Israel, who had also railed against the oppressive rich." When studying Scripture, I typically use *The HarperCollins Study Bible*. In the subject heading for 5:1-6 *The HarperCollins Study Bible* has: "Warning to Rich Oppressors."[11] Again, James's target is not economic blessedness itself, with which a thoughtful and generous steward can do great good. It is the oppressiveness, the carelessness in the deepest sense of the word, of people who *have* vis-à-vis those who *have not* that is under judgment here.

N. T. Wright observes: "...the church must keep James 5:1-6 at its elbow...."[12] As I write this meditation, my elbow is close to my body. James 5:1-6 is not just for first-century Palestine, says Wright. The church of today must keep its teaching at its elbow. Ralph Martin writes: "James stirs the social conscience by denouncing the mock piety of those who make pretense of 'calling upon God' in worship, when the only voice that reaches to heaven is the cry of the oppressed workers who have been cheated out of their daily wages."[13] When we 'cry to heaven' in worship, that worship is meant to be sincere, heartfelt, and such worship will hear the cries of the poor and generate a response of compassion and generosity.

In conclusion, I go back to James 1:27: "Religion that is pure and undefiled before God, the Father, is this: to care for orphans and widows in their distress, and to keep oneself unstained by the world." Here we have one of the most memorable passages in James. "Orphans and widows" in 1:27 is an umbrella term. The term goes back to the Old Testament. "Orphans and widows" represent those who are most vulnerable in society. And the day laborers in 5:4 fall into that category. Thus 5:1-6 is directly related to 1:27: "Religion that is pure and undefiled before God, the Father, is this: to care for orphans and widows..." *and* day laborers—and all who have none to care for them. This is true religion, to be good and grateful and generous stewards of God's blessings, so that those blessings can be dispersed, shared, claimed by and transformative for those who have previously been powerless.

A careful reading of James does indeed 'stir the social conscience.' This moment in history is, of all moments, a time for our social consciences to be stirred. This moment in history necessitates deep soul-searching for us as individuals, as members of the church, and as citizens of our country. To miss this prompting would be to miss the moment. A thoughtful reading of James does indeed stir our social conscience. Which calls to mind 5:4: "Listen!" Amen.

PATIENCE AND ENDURANCE

JAMES 5:7-11 • 10 SEPTEMBER 2020

⁷Be patient, therefore, beloved, until the coming of the Lord. The farmer waits for the precious crop from the earth, being patient with it until it receives the early and the late rains. ⁸You also must be patient. Strengthen your hearts, for the coming of the Lord is near. ⁹Beloved, do not grumble against one another, so that you may not be judged. See, the Judge is standing at the doors! ¹⁰As an example of suffering and patience, beloved, take the prophets who spoke in the name of the Lord. ¹¹Indeed we call blessed those who showed endurance. You have heard of the endurance of Job, and you have seen the purpose of the Lord, how the Lord is compassionate and merciful.

James 5:7-11 marks the beginning of the conclusion of the epistle. The passage deals with patience and endurance, and in James these words fit together like hand and glove. For James, patience and endurance are closely related. At the very beginning of the epistle, 1:2-3, James deals with patience and endurance, and now as he begins to draw the letter to a close, he revisits their importance. The preceding passage, 5:1-6, deals with the oppression of poor workers. James has taken on the systemic mistreatment of the most vulnerable in 5:1-6, and the tone shifts now in 5:7-11 as does the target audience. In 5:7-11, James resumes addressing members of a Christian congregation, many of whom, no doubt, live on the margins of society and are among the very poor—people who on a daily basis struggle to make ends meet.

Verse 7 begins: "Be patient, therefore, beloved...." James is once again addressing his readers as family. "Be patient, therefore...." The Greek for "therefore" connects the passage to verses 1-6. Having taken on the powerful, James now speaks directly to those who are oppressed. Be patient, therefore, *beloved....* The Greek actually reads *adelphoi,* brothers. Thus, once again, James is addressing family, *siblings* in the faith. And it is a very warm address. The immediate cause for patience in this passage is the *parousia,* the "coming of the Lord (v. 8)." Early Christians lived in the hope that the risen Christ would return to earth sooner rather than later.

It is understandable that members of the early church were fixated on 'when' regarding the *parousia,* the second coming. Even in 2020 there are Christians in certain traditions who remain fixated, ever trusting that the event will happen *soon.* James counsels against this kind of fixation, even in the first century. "Be patient, therefore, beloved," he writes, "until the coming of the Lord." And then he uses the analogy of farming. A farmer, for all of his or her hard work in the meantime, must ultimately have patience regarding the harvest. The farmer works to plant, to water, to weed, to cultivate, but in the end has to be patient and wait for the desired result.

In his commentary on 5:7-11, N. T. Wright observes: "... patience is one of the key aspects of the spirit's work in our lives."[1] We all want patience, don't we? And we want it now! Wright adds: "Our frantic modern society...has done its best to obliterate the need for patience."[2] We simply do not wait well, we modern folk—particularly we Westerners. We want what we want and we want it now. That said, James's counsel here is timeless. *We* need to hear this message every bit as much as did his original audience. Sometimes in life we simply have to be patient. Some things just take time. And oftentimes the timing is out of our control, and if we can come to peace with this and accept it, rather than making ourselves increasingly anxious about *when*, then we are all the better for it. Patience is clearly a virtue, for which James is a passionate and articulate advocate.

David Nystrom notes that 5:7-11 is: "...a call to patient living under adverse circumstances."[3] It is clear contextually that at least some of the congregation to whom James was writing would have been people on the margins of society, the very poor, day laborers and their families. Nearly 2,000 years later, James's message is timely in the midst of a global pandemic the likes of which the world has not faced in 100 years.

Regarding the delay of the *parousia*, Nystrom observes that James is saying to his readers: "...every day ought to be lived with the same devotion to Christian principles and morals as if it were the last day."[4] Rather than waiting passively and anxiously regarding the 'when' of Christ's return, James's counsel is to live each day to the full and not take on needless stress over something beyond one's control. Nystrom's wording is particularly instructive: "...*every day* (emphasis mine) ought to be lived with the same devotion to Christian principles and morals as if it were the last day."

During this time of pandemic, when we are all struggling with how to deal with COVID-19, in my own spiritual life I have come to a deeper place of gratitude for the *gift* of another day, the gift of basic good health. As I was preparing this meditation I thought to myself: "I knew this, intellectually, *before* the pandemic. At an intellectual level, I knew to be grateful." And indeed I have made significant progress over the years in being increasingly grateful for 'simple' blessings. But the pandemic has pushed me to a deeper level with regard to my own sense of gratitude. James has a great lesson for us here in 5:7-11 as well as for his original audience. If we can live each day with the same principles, the same guiding spirit, and recognize each day for the gift that it is we are so much the better for it.

Then verse 9: "Beloved, do not grumble against one another, so that you may not be judged. See the Judge is standing at the doors!" The real judge is nearby, and thus *we* are not meant to be the judge of others. In 4:11-12, James has written specifically about the danger of brothers and sisters in Christ standing in judgment of one another. This theme is revisited in 5:9 as the epistle begins to draw to a close. We in the Christian family are not to stand in judgment of each other. We are sisters and brothers of equal standing in the eyes of God, and are therefore meant to have equal standing with each other. James's conviction is based on the teaching of Jesus, so compellingly and concisely articulated in Matthew 7:1: "Do not judge, so that you may not be judged." The baseline teaching of Jesus cannot be clearer: Judge not. In their commentary on 5:9, Craig Blomberg and Mariam Kamell write: "Criticizing others implies judging them...."[5] A spirit of criticism is, in the end, a spirit of judgment. And even if the facts are clear and on our side, when we hold ourselves up over against other people, consciously or unconsciously, we are judging them.

Luke Timothy Johnson writes about 5:9: "As always, James advocates solidarity."[6] What an insightful, concise summary statement. And of all times, now is a time for people in Christian communities to remember the solidarity that we are to have with each other. Especially now, in the midst of the pandemic, we really are "all in this together" and are always to be looking to support one another in the faith.

James is primarily a moral theologian. James overtly addresses the subject of right and wrong. And James is ever a practical theologian. Everything James writes is meant to be usable in daily life—in the first century and ours. David Nystrom writes in summary regarding 5:9: "Life does bring trials, of course, but no one is served by the cultivation of a spirit of complaining."[7] This is one of those truisms that could be taped to the bathroom mirror, or to the back of a door. I have all kinds of quotations on the back of my office door so that I can see them and be reminded of them frequently. Nystrom provides an arrestingly clear summary statement on 5:9: Even amidst life's trials, no one is served by the cultivation of a spirit of complaining.

Then verse 10: "As an example of suffering and patience, beloved, take the prophets who spoke in the name of the Lord." Have you ever noticed that prophets are always more popular after they are dead? It is a really clear trend. Prophets poll higher after they are dead! Jesus himself experienced rejection, even in his hometown, and at first even among his own family. Of course, it is he who observed: "Prophets are not without honor, except in their hometown, and among their own kin, and in their own house."[8]

Prophets are more beloved in hindsight than in real time. By the time James was writing in the Christian era, the prophets of the Old Testament had become truly revered. By the first century there had been a dearth of prophecy in the Jewish tradition for generations. It was thought that the prophetic line had ended, and this is one of the reasons why John the Baptist generated so much interest and controversy, as people recognized the prophetic nature of his proclamation. Jesus arrives and John *proclaims* Jesus as being even greater than he. By the time of James's writing, prophets in the Jewish tradition who may have been bitterly divisive in their own time have, in retrospect, come to be revered.

Hindsight is 20/20. James lifts up the examples of the prophets, and here Sophie Laws observes: "James reminds his readers of the high regard in which perseverance is familiarly held...."[9] With the benefit of hindsight, prophets had come to be seen as models of perseverance, endurance, and faithfulness. Along this line, Kurt Richardson writes: "In many ways endurance was James's chief virtue of faith."[10] Again, how timely is this message? To be patient, to be strong in a time of trial—to endure. Nothing is more important for James or, by extension, for us.

In verse 11 we read: "Indeed we call blessed those who showed endurance. You have heard of the endurance of Job...." Most of us know the phrase: "the patience of Job." Job's legacy was reflected upon by the rabbis long after the Book of Job itself was written. Even in the time of James, rabbis were still adding to the body of work on Job. Indeed, a rabbinic text on Job is thought to have been written nearly contemporaneously with the Epistle of James, the essential point here being that the theological significance of Job was still on the increase generations after the Book of Job had come into widespread use. Ralph Martin writes in his commentary regarding the reference to Job in 5:11: "Patience is not quietism...."[11] This is particularly important for a proper interpretation of James. James's counsel to patience does not mean that we are to sit quietly or passively. Patience in James has the connotation of endurance, of being strong in a time of trial. William Barclay reflects on James's reference to Job: "Job's is no unquestioning submission; he struggled and questioned, and sometimes even defied, but the flame of his faith was never extinguished."[12]

Job was not a passive victim. He questioned and struggled. He was more than able to speak up for himself, but in the end his faith remained, and thus he is held up by James in the first century of the Christian era as one of the great examples of the kind of patience and endurance advocated in the epistle. On this note, David Nystrom writes: "...as was the case with Job and the prophets, our character is forged on the anvil of difficulty."[13]

Just consider the timeliness of James's wisdom for our situation, this difficult time in our cultural history. I do not know anyone who does not enjoy a season in which one is relatively carefree and 'everything' is going well. I do not know anyone who does not enjoy such times if we are graced even to have them. But when we think about it, it really is in life's more difficult times that our character is forged. It is in and through challenging times that we grow stronger and more resilient. Kent Hughes observes: "...our moral development—our character—is largely dependent upon the experience of suffering...the study of the lives of great people reveals there is a consistent link between the crucible and true greatness. No wise person would seek to be exempt from the healthy discipline of trouble."[14] Down deep we know this to be true, and though we would not *choose* times of struggle, it is in such times that our character is formed and strengthened. It is through times of struggle, when we persevere and come through them, that we emerge the wiser for them. Typically it is through such times that we become more compassionate and more humble. More often than not, it is through times of struggle that we are pushed forward in our character development and in our spiritual development. Thus, even in the midst of this pandemic, and in the midst of all the cultural upheaval that we are experiencing, even now we are wise to be looking for the lessons to be learned. How can this time be redeemed? What are the lessons from this season that we are meant to learn? And what lessons learned can we take from this time and apply moving forward?

Still in verse 11, James writes: "You have heard of the endurance of Job, and you have seen the purpose of the Lord, how the Lord is compassionate and merciful." The prophets called God's covenant people to return to compassion, sensitivity, and an awareness of the poor as God's beloved. The prophets call *us* back to a life of compassion and mercy. James concludes this section of his epistle reminding us that such is the nature of God. In the Judeo-Christian tradition, God's essence is compassion and mercy.

Commenting on verse 11, N. T Wright observes: "God's mercy is sovereign. That is the deepest truth about him."[15] We worship a merciful God. The English priest and spiritual writer Michael Mayne frequently observed that God's judgment is always more than matched by his mercy. We worship a loving God whose very nature is compassion. Aída Besançon Spencer writes in her commentary on this passage: "God's very nature is deep compassion."[16] Here we are reminded of Exodus 34, when Moses is on Mount Sinai experiencing the presence and spirit of God. In Exodus 34:6 we read: "...a God merciful and gracious, slow to anger, and abounding in steadfast love and faithfulness...." In the end, all of James's pastoral teaching is meant to remind us that we serve a God who is compassionate and merciful.

Among all of the Gospel writers, Luke is the one who is most at pains to remind us of God's compassion. To be sure, Matthew, Mark, and John also clearly depict a compassionate, merciful God. But Luke is more intentional than any of the other Gospel writers about framing the nature of God, and the nature of Jesus himself, in terms of compassion for those on the margins of society: those who are poor, those who are hurting, those who are struggling. Jesus is quintessentially a person of compassion, and his compassion mirrors God's compassion. It is only in Luke 6:36 that we read this precise statement: "Be merciful, just as your Father is merciful." This is the God whom James is calling us to remember, praise, and serve. The Greek for "merciful" can also be translated as "compassionate." "Be compassionate, just as your Father is compassionate." Amen.

A RICH TREASURY OF PRAISE

JAMES 5:13-16 • 17 SEPTEMBER 2020

[13]Are any among you suffering? They should pray. Are any cheerful? They should sing songs of praise. [14]Are any among you sick? They should call for the elders of the church and have them pray over them, anointing them with oil in the name of the Lord. [15]The prayer of faith will save the sick, and the Lord will raise them up; and anyone who has committed sins will be forgiven. [16]Therefore confess yours sins to one another, and pray for one another, so that you may be healed. The prayer of the righteous is powerful and effective.

In her commentary on 5:13-14, Marie Isaacs writes: "Nowhere is the pastoral orientation of James more evident than in this concluding section."[1] This is James at his pastoral best, offering instruction on the church's life in community.

In 5:13-14 James writes: "Are any among you suffering? They should pray. Are any cheerful? They should sing songs of praise. Are any among you sick? They should call for the elders of the church and have them pray over them...." Prayer is the foundation of the church's life. Even if I were not an Episcopal priest, I would still say that the definition of prayer in *The Book of Common Prayer* is the best definition of prayer I have ever known. In the Catechism, the Prayer Book teaches: "Prayer is responding to God, by thought and by deeds, with or without words."[2]

In commenting on verses 13-14, N. T. Wright observes: "Prayer must surround everything else that we do, whether sad or happy, suffering or cheerful."[3] Everything that we do as Christians is to be grounded in, and guided by, prayer. Kent Hughes writes in commenting on the passage: "...all of life is to be bathed in prayer...."[4] In welcoming a new season of Lent and its promise of forgiveness and reconciliation, an Episcopal bishop wrote to his diocese: "Bathe in God's love."

Once again the definition of prayer: "...responding to God, by thought and by deeds, with or without words." We are to have a prayerful spirit at all times. Of course, we cannot be on our knees at all times! And only so many of us are called to be monks or nuns. Only so many of us are called to be pastors. But we *all* can cultivate a prayerful spirit. We all are called to live our lives in response to God: in our thinking, and in our actions.

Ralph Martin observes regarding 5:13-16: "...the reader enters a world of congregational relationships which embrace the entire spectrum of life's experiences, extending from gladness to sadness."[5] Just think about the life experience in any congregation, of any size, and the range of emotions that parishioners have experienced over the years. I have been struck over my years in pastoral ministry by how many times a pre-baptism meeting with a joyful family has been directly followed by a funeral planning meeting with a grieving family. This has happened *many* times over the years. The same can be said regarding a pre-marital counseling session vis-à-vis meeting with a bereaved family for funeral planning. As I was preparing this very meditation in an atmosphere of peace and tranquility, the office called notifying me of a pastoral emergency.

We are always experiencing a range of circumstances and emotions. This is the stuff of life: it is the human condition. Norman Vincent Peale, pastor and bestselling spiritual writer, once observed that we should never miss an opportunity to express our sympathy with a fellow church member who is hurting, and we should never miss an opportunity to share our happiness with a fellow church member who is joyful. As members of a Christian family, we are to be prepared to experience and acknowledge the entire range of life experiences and emotions, from gladness to sadness. The joys of life we should celebrate! And the sadnesses we must observe and respect and be willing to help people through such times. Normal Vincent Peale, as lastingly influential a figure as he is, did not invent this theology. Paul writes in Romans 12:15: "Rejoice with those who rejoice, weep with those who weep."

In his commentary on 5:13-16, James Adamson notes: "This passage...shows that from the earliest days the church possessed a rich treasury of praise."[6] It is crucially important for us to remember some 2,000 years out from its birth that the church's founding was grounded squarely on Easter. The church existed, and exists today, to proclaim the reality of Easter. The theologian Martin Kähler once observed: "To state the matter somewhat provocatively, one could call the Gospels passion narratives with extended introductions."[7]

William Barclay writes regarding 5:13-16: "There was joy in the hearts of the Christians which burst from their lips in songs of praise for the mercy and the grace of God."[8] He adds: "...in the Christian Church, from the beginning until now, there has been the music of praise, for Christians remember an infinite love and enjoy a present glory."[9] The *present glory* is Christ risen and active. Day by day, week by week, in Christian churches the world over, as the Eucharistic Prayer unfolds there are repeated references to Easter. *The* reason for the church to exist is to proclaim the present glory: Christ is risen! Christ is with us. He has been with us from the beginning of this pandemic. He is with us in this season of social unrest and awakening. Our present glory, in all times and in all places, is the presence of Christ.

It is extraordinary to realize how relevant James is to life in 2020. A nearly 2,000 year old Christian text is as relevant today as it was when it was written. And yet, we do live in a very different time and a very different culture, two millennia removed from the original historical context of the Epistle of James. On this note, David Nystrom writes: "We inhabit a social and cultural world in which a great premium is placed on the elimination of discomfort."[10] Let's just think about that for a moment. We do not like discomfort, do we? I remember a night a couple of years ago when I had drifted off to sleep on the couch, and as I woke up at about 2:00 a.m. there was a late-night infomercial on pushing a product (a pill) that would enable dramatic and sustainable weight loss with *no change in diet* and *no increase in exercise*! This speaks to a culture that does not like discomfort. We have medicines for very nearly everything. To be sure, I take them when I need them. Thank God for modern medicine.

The pandemic has created a spike in anxieties through the uncertainties that it has brought and the fear that it has generated. These are real and understandable reactions. And yet, even in the midst of this pandemic we are wise to consider how blessed we are to live in a time and in a culture with so many resources that we can bring to bear to combat not only the medical realities of the pandemic, but the social and psychological dislocation as well.

Think about how many resources we have at our disposal in facing the pandemic that so many people around the world simply do not have. Imagine being of age in 1918 and facing that pandemic without the resources that we can bring to bear today. All of which is to say that, even in difficult moments, as Christians we are yet to look for blessings. We are to look for and claim and be thankful for, and then share as we are able, so many blessings that so many others cannot even imagine. Every blessing that we have is a gift, and James encourages us: When you are sad, pray. When you are sick, pray. But also, when you are cheerful *remember* to sing songs of praise. Recognize blessings, 'small' and great. Claim them. Share them. And remember always, they come from God. "Every generous act of giving, with every perfect gift, is from above, coming down from the Father of lights, with whom there is no variation or shadow due to change (1:17)." Paul puts it: "Rejoice always, pray without ceasing, give thanks in all circumstances; for this is the will of God in Christ Jesus for you."[11] Amen.

A SUMMONS TO ACTION

JAMES 5:17-20 • 24 SEPTEMBER 2020

¹⁷Elijah was a human being like us, and he prayed fervently that it might not rain, and for three years and six months it did not rain on the earth. ¹⁸Then he prayed again, and the heaven gave rain and the earth yielded its harvest. ¹⁹My brothers and sisters, if anyone among you wanders from the truth and is brought back by another, ²⁰ you should know that whoever brings back a sinner from wandering will save the sinner's soul from death and will cover a multitude of sins.

The final section of the Epistle of James is 5:13-20, which subdivides between verses 13-16 and 17-20. In 5:13-16, James addresses the importance of prayer to the life of the Christian community. A community of faith is first and foremost a praying community. Commenting on James's sense of communal prayer, Dan McCartney writes: "...it is the faithful *community* whose prayer may be regarded as powerful and effective."[1]

So 5:13-16 deals with prayer, and then the argument moves forward beginning in verse 17, where James writes: "Elijah was a human being like us...." Here we meet the fourth hero from the Hebrew Scriptures in the Epistle of James. For James, these four exemplars are models to the Christian community of faithfulness. We meet Abraham in 2:21-24, Rahab in 2:25, and Job in 5:11. Now in 5:17 we meet Elijah. By the New Testament era, no figure in the Hebrew Scriptures other than Moses was more revered than Elijah. The two *great* figures of the Old Testament by the New Testament era were Moses and Elijah. We can see this clearly in the event of the Transfiguration.[2] When Jesus is on the mountaintop, out of all the great characters of the Hebrew Scriptures, he is joined by only two: Moses and Elijah. As James was writing his epistle, Elijah was of great, lasting, and still growing significance as a hero of the ancient faith tradition of Judaism.

"Elijah was a human being like us...." In commenting on 5:17, Luke Timothy Johnson writes: "...emphasizing the humanity of Elijah functions to affirm the possibilities available to them [members of the community] in their prayers."[3] Johnson emphasizes here that James is intentional about making sure that people remember that Elijah was, in fact, a human being. Aída Besançon Spencer notes in her commentary: "...James wants to encourage the praying community to identify with Elijah, not treat him as uniquely gifted."[4] In commending the faithfulness of Elijah to his readers, James is intentional in reminding them that Elijah was like them, and thus they can be like him in faithfulness. "Elijah was a human being like us, and he prayed fervently...."

The last subsection of the epistle is 5:19-20. James begins this subsection as he has several other times: "My brothers and sisters...." Here, once again, James speaks to the importance of the community of faith understanding itself as family, family in the best sense of the term. And in that family there is to be solidarity. Of course, there will be moments when opinions differ. And, to be sure, there will be personality conflicts as there always are when humans come together and interact with each other. But, in the end, the church is to be a place where members treat each other as family, and work toward a loving, cohesive, mutually supportive unity. James models this sense of sibling relationship by introducing sections of teaching with: "My brothers and sisters...."

Tradition holds that the James of this epistle is St. James of Jerusalem—James, the brother of Jesus. We know historically that James served as pastor over the Christian church in Jerusalem.[5] Even James, *the brother of Jesus* and chief pastor of the emerging Jerusalem church—even James understands that *all* members of the worshiping community are siblings, sisters and brothers in the faith.

What does James deal with in this final subsection? Luke Timothy Johnson calls it "fraternal correction."[6] We modern interpreters have to be careful with this last subsection of James. We live in a culture marked by a default assumption of individualism. We live in a time when the assumption of privacy is of utmost concern to people. We just assume that people should respect our personal space, and our personal lives. We sometimes refer to our "bubble," a literal sense of our personal space. James wrote in a very different time. In the biblical era people had to depend on each other for the basic necessities of life. People bartered for goods and services. All facets of community life were interrelated. People living in such close community had to be able to get along because they had to depend on each other. In the time period in which James was writing it was perfectly normal for one friend to say to another: "Really?" People in the ancient world were not as hesitant as we are in offering their opinions to each other because then it was simply part of what friendship meant. While some of our friends may still feel this way(!), such actions are definitely counter-cultural. But in the biblical era it would have made perfect sense for one member of the community to correct another; the concept of friendship was supported by a different paradigm than our modern understanding. By the same token, philosophers and other teachers existed to point people in the right direction, and part of the teaching office was to point out when those in their charge were headed in the wrong direction. We see evidence of this in the Gospels in the Parable of the Lost Sheep, Matthew 18:10-14. The parable itself is followed in verses 15-20 by a block of teaching on disciplining members of the church, which involves members 'pointing out the faults' of their peers.

In interpreting this final subsection of James, we simply have to be aware as moderns that we bring a different worldview to the material. To this end Luke Timothy Johnson observes: "This final example of plain speech in the community is perhaps most offensive to contemporary groups in which the strange ethos has taken root that regards every opinion as worthy of consideration and every behavior tolerable."[7] These days, everyone gets a trophy. We Westerners do not react well when people give us unsolicited advice—at least most of us do not react well most of the time. On a personal note, I can be just as unappreciative as anyone else of unsolicited advice! Johnson here insightfully cautions us that we must hear James's counsel in verses 19-20 in historical context.

"My brothers and sisters, if anyone among you wanders from the truth...." Our attention might go immediately to the idea of "wandering," and yet let us not lose sight of the word "truth." James is preeminently a moral theologian concerned with right behavior, behavior that is grounded in spiritual principles. James's concern here is the prospect of people drifting from the truth. His concern is, in the end, pastoral, and is grounded in compassion. This line of pastoral teaching is not about controlling other people's lives, but is instead geared toward helping people make the best decisions possible. Ralph Martin comments here: "...truth is something [for James] that is to be 'done' as well as believed...."[8] James has made clear throughout the epistle that anything we believe in theologically is to be made manifest in how we conduct ourselves. Thus members of the community, says James, need to be willing and able to lead other members of the community back to the truth.

A study note in *The HarperCollins Study Bible* reads: "As in the OT wisdom literature, *wisdom* [for James] is associated with practical good behavior, not speculative thought."[9] It has been emphasized several times in this series of meditations that James is always about practical wisdom. James offers spiritual guidance that is applicable to daily life. It was true for his original audience, and it is true for us. James's every word can be applied to daily living.

With regard to this section on community, Pheme Perkins writes: "All members have a responsibility to aid one another in the trials of life."[10] As moderns we may have a little bit of pushback against the details of what James says here. But, in the end, what he is concerned with is the well-being of the community. Both then and now, members of a faith community are to be attentive to each other's needs to help foster the well-being and solidarity of the community.

From early on in the pandemic, we were careful to say in all communications from the church office regarding our suspension of in-person worship: If you are concerned about someone in the church community, give them a call. If you are wondering how someone is doing, call them. Send them an e-mail. Send them a text message. Drop them a note in the mail. In the end, our pastoral approach during the pandemic was and is simple: Care for one another.

What James is ultimately getting at here in the final subsection of the epistle is the importance of fostering healthy, meaningful relationships within community. "My brothers and sisters, if anyone among you wanders from the truth...." In reflecting on verses 19-20, in addition to being concerned about when others wander, it is important for us to remember our own potential to wander. We all can drift from best practices. We all can realize at some point: I'm off the path. I have not been living my life in accord with my highest spiritual principles. Contextually, James's concern is to offer encouragement to members of the community who may have wandered from the truth. Equally important to us as we read James from our own context is recognition of our own tendency to wander. And when we come to the realization: 'It is I...,' we are to have the humility to seek and welcome forgiveness, and then come back to where we know we are meant to be as a beloved member of our faith community. So much that underlies James's teaching is his advocacy of a baseline humility, and that call to humility is subtly yet powerfully present in verses 19-20.

In the era in which James wrote, letters typically were concluded with greetings and blessings. We see that very clearly in Paul's letters. Typically in Paul's letters the ending includes a series of greetings, and then a blessing, a benediction. But not so with James. James's letter does not conclude in a typical fashion for its time frame. Douglas Moo observes on this note: "James does not conclude his letter with greetings and benedictions typical of epistolary endings, but with a summons to action."[11] James *is James* to the very end of the epistle. Even the epistle's last verse is a call to action. Moo continues: "...there are more imperative verbs per word in James than in any other NT book."[12] Throughout, James is fundamentally a call to action, grounded in and guided by the faith that is in us.

It has long been recognized in scholarly circles that while James is written in the form of a letter, the text actually functions as a sermon. The platform, the framework of the sermon is in the *form* of a letter. The Epistle of James is really a sermon, and considered in that light, James is one of the great sermons in all of Christian history. In terms of the New Testament itself, if we regard James's epistle as a sermon it belongs in a category alongside Jesus's own Sermon on the Mount (Matthew 5:1-7:24). We have that great sermon from Jesus; we have Luke's version of that sermon as well (Luke 6:20-49), and in the Epistle of James we have from Jesus's own brother one of the great sermons from earliest Christianity. Regarding James's letter not ending in a typical epistolary way, Ralph Martin observes: "...a closing section like vv 19-20 matches exactly the rugged and forceful style hitherto displayed."[13] James is *James* to the very end, a prophet calling the people of God to concrete, Godly actions in the world.

This series of weekly meditations on James began in response to the global pandemic. During this time frame we then have experienced the deaths of Ahmaud Arbery, George Floyd, and other cultural moments that have led to much social stirring, ongoing social protests, and a long overdue time of soul-searching in this nation. During the preparation of this final meditation, the Attorney General of Kentucky was holding a press conference regarding the Breonna Taylor case. This deep dive into James has not been offered as a means of escape from the realities with which we are dealing. In no way has this series of meditations been meant as a means of 'escape' from reality. To the contrary, this deep dive into James is meant as a way *into* reality, a substantive means of addressing head on this time of uncertainty that we are in, and the social and cultural challenges that are squarely before us.

Over the years I have said on occasion, long before this series of meditations was ever in view, that James is as practical a book as any in the canon of Scripture. James has application in every arena of life. This series of meditations, offered in the context of liturgy, has been meant to equip us to face up to this time, to meet this moment head on, and to apply in our daily living the faith that is in us. As James meant for his original audience, now his epistle is meant to guide us in putting into practice our highest theological and spiritual principles. To this end, with 1:18 in mind, Luke Timothy Johnson notes: "A community taking its lead from James can indeed be a 'kind of first fruits' of God's creatures."[14] Amen.

ACKNOWLEDGMENTS

My thanks to all who heard the original offering of these meditations on Facebook, and for your thoughtful and encouraging comments. Thanks to Isaac Doty for his expert facilitation of each live-streamed service. Thanks to Andrea Spraggins for her diligence in typing the original version of these meditations for the parish archive. Thanks to Liz Turpin for her faithful service as lector and 'congregation' throughout the entire fifteen-week series. Liz, you know your James! Thanks to John R. Mabry of The Apocryphile Press for his interest in and support of this project, and to Rob Gieselmann for pointing me in John's direction. Thanks to Carl Holladay, Brian Cole, Mark Chapman, Mark Oakley, and Joan Cronan for your gracious support of this book, and for our friendship.

Thanks to my parents, Pansy and Joe Huffstetler, for instilling in me a love of Scripture and the recognition of its primacy. Thanks to Alison Mayne for your encouragement and support for more than a decade, and for our friendship. Alison, in tending Michael's voice I found my own.

Finally, thanks to my wife Debbie, who has partnered with

me at every stage of this project, including offering invaluable editorial assistance, and typing numerous versions of the 'final' draft. Thank you, my love. In the end, I did this for you.

NOTES

PREFACE

1. Sophie Laws, "The Letter of James." *The HarperCollins Study Bible* (New Revised Standard Version). Wayne A. Meeks, General Editor (New York: HarperCollins, Publishers, Inc., 1993), 2269.
2. *Ibid.*, 2270.
3. Carl R. Holladay, *Introduction to the New Testament*. Reference Edition (Waco, TX: Baylor University Press, 2017), 745.
4. Luke Timothy Johnson, "James." *Harper's Bible Commentary*. James L. Mays, General Editor (San Francisco: Harper and Row, Publishers, 1988), 1272.

1. PRACTICAL FAITH AND ACTIVE LOVE

1. Sophie Laws, *The Epistle of James*. Harper's New Testament Commentaries. Henry Chadwick, General Editor (San Francisco: Harper and Row, Publishers, 1980), 53.
2. Peter H. Davids, *James*. New International Biblical Commentary. W. Ward Gasque, New Testament Editor (Peabody, MA: Hendrickson Publishers, Inc., 1989), 27.
3. Ralph P. Martin, *James*. Word Biblical Commentary, Volume 48. David A. Hubbard and Glenn W. Barker, General Editors (Waco, TX: Word, 1988), 17.
4. Luke Timothy Johnson, "James." *Harper's Bible Commentary*. James L. Mays, General Editor (San Francisco: Harper and Row, Publishers, 1988), 1272.
5. *Ibid.*

2. OUR TIME AND PLACE

1. *The Book of Common Prayer* (New York: The Seabury Press, 1979), 13.
2. Luke Timothy Johnson, *The Letter of James: A New Translation with Introduction and Commentary*. The Anchor Bible, Volume 37A. William Foxwell Albright and David Noel Freedman, General Editors (New York: Doubleday, 1995), 204.

3. THE IMPORTANCE OF LISTENING

1. R. Kent Hughes, *James: Faith That Works*. Preaching the Word, Volume 6 (Wheaton, IL: Crossway Books, 1991), 63.
2. Craig L. Blomberg and Mariam J. Kamell, *James*. Zondervan Exegetical Commentary on the New Testament, Volume 16. Clinton E. Arnold, General Editor (Grand Rapids, MI: Zondervan, 2008), 85.
3. Kurt A. Richardson, *James: An Exegetical and Theological Exposition of Holy Scripture*. The New American Commentary, Volume 36. E. Ray Clendenen, General Editor (Nashville: Broadman and Holman Publishers, 1997), 88.
4. Dan G. McCartney, *James*. Baker Exegetical Commentary on the New Testament. Robert W. Yarbrough and Robert H. Stein, Editors (Grant Rapids, MI: Baker Academic, 2009), 116.
5. Hughes, 66.
6. Ralph P. Martin, *James*. Word Biblical Commentary, Volume 48. David A. Hubbard and Glenn W. Barker, General Editors (Waco, TX: Word, 1988), 49.

4. A TIME OF SOUL-SEARCHING

1. Douglas J. Moo, *The Letter of James*. The Pillar New Testament Commentary. D. A. Carson, General Editor (Grand Rapids, MI: William B. Eerdmans Publishing Company, 2000), 89.
2. Luke Timothy Johnson, "James." *Harper's Bible Commentary*. James L. Mays, General Editor (San Francisco: Harper and Row, Publishers, 1988), 1273.
3. William Barclay, *The New Daily Study Bible: The Letters of James and Peter*. Linda Foster, Editor (Louisville, KY: Westminster John Knox Press, 2003), 68.
4. Kurt A. Richardson, *James*. The New American Commentary, Volume 36. E. Ray Clendenen, General Editor (Nashville: Broadman and Holman Publishers, 1977), 94.
5. *The Book of Common Prayer* (New York: The Seabury Press, 1979), 17.
6. *Ibid.*, 25.
7. *Ibid.*, 258.

5. STICKS AND STONES

1. Dan G. McCartney, *James*. Baker Exegetical Commentary on the New Testament. Robert W. Yarbrough and Robert H. Stein, Editors (Grand Rapids, MI: Baker Academic, 2009), 128.
2. Kurt A. Richardson, *James: An Exegetical and Theological Exposition of Holy Scripture*. The New American Commentary, Volume 36. E. Ray Clendenen, General Editor (Nashville: Broadman and Holman Publishers, 1997), 99.

3. Marie E. Isaacs, *Reading Hebrews and James: A Literary and Theological Commentary*. Reading the New Testament. Charles H. Talbert, General Editor (Macon, GA: Smyth and Helwys Publishing, Inc., 2002), 194.

4. Luke Timothy Johnson, *The Letter of James: A New Translation with Introduction and Commentary*. The Anchor Bible, Volume 37A. William Foxwell Albright and David Noel Freedman, General Editors (New York: Doubleday, 1995), 212.

5. *Webster's Ninth New Collegiate Dictionary* (Springfield, MA: Merriam-Webster, Inc., Publishers, 1987), 410.

6. *Ibid.*

7. Richardson, 102.

8. Ralph P. Martin, *James*. Word Biblical Commentary, Volume 48. David A. Hubbard and Glenn W. Barker, General Editors (Waco, TX: Word, 1988), 54.

6. THE SIN OF DISCRIMINATION

1. R. Kent Hughes, *James: Faith that Works*. Preaching the Word (Wheaton, IL: Crossway Books, 1991), 98.

2. *Webster's Ninth New Collegiate Dictionary* (Springfield, MA: Merriam-Webster, Inc., 1987), 771.

3. Luke Timothy Johnson, *The Letter of James: A New Translation with Introduction and Commentary*. The Anchor Bible, Volume 37A. William Foxwell Albright and David Noel Freedman, General Editors (New York: Doubleday, 1995), 226.

4. Johnson, "James." *Harper's Bible Commentary*. James L. Mays, General Editor (San Francisco: Harper and Row, Publishers, 1988), 1273.

5. Johnson, *The Letter of James*, 227.

6. James B. Adamson, *The Epistle of James*. The New International Commentary on the New Testament. F. F. Bruce, Editor (Grand Rapids, MI: William B. Eerdmans Publishing Company, 1976), 107.

7. John Keats, letter to George and Georgiana Keats, February 14, 1818.

8. Sophie Laws, *The Epistle of James*. Harper's New Testament Commentaries. Henry Chadwick, General Editor (San Francisco: Harper and Row, Publishers, 1980), 93.

9. Dan G. McCartney, *James*. Baker Exegetical Commentary on the New Testament. Robert W. Yarbrough and Robert H. Stein, Editors (Grand Rapids, MI: Baker Academic, 2009), 134.

7. I WILL, WITH GOD'S HELP

1. *The Book of Common Prayer* (New York: The Seabury Press, 1979), 305.

2. *Ibid.*

3. *Ibid.*

4. Solomon Andria. "James." *Africa Bible Commentary*. Tokunboh Adeyemo, General Editor (Grand Rapids, MI: Zondervan, 2006), 1538.

5. *Ibid.*

6. Luke Timothy Johnson, *The Letter of James: A New Translation with Introduction and Commentary*. The Anchor Bible, Volume 37A. William Foxwell Albright and David Noel Freedman, General Editors (New York: Doubleday, 1995), 247.

7. *Ibid.*, 239.

8. Dan G. McCartney, *James*. Baker Exegetical Commentary on the New Testament. Robert W. Yarbrough and Robert H. Stein, Editors (Grand Rapids, MI: Baker Academic, 2009), 156.

9. *Webster's Ninth New Collegiate Dictionary* (Springfield, MA: Merriam-Webster, Inc., 1987), 410.

8. IS IT LOVING?

1. R. Kent Hughes, *James: Faith That Works*. Preaching the Word (Wheaton, IL: Crossway Books, 1991), 143.

2. *Ibid.*

3. Pheme Perkins, *First and Second Peter, James, and Jude*. Interpretation: A Bible Commentary for Teaching and Preaching. James Luther Mays, Editor (Louisville, KY: Westminster John Knox Press, 1995), 120.

4. Hughes, 142.

5. William Barclay, *The New Daily Study Bible: The Letters of James and Peter*. Linda Foster, Editor (Louisville, KY: Westminster John Knox Press, 2003), 104.

6. Luke Timothy Johnson, *The Letter of James: A New Translation with Introduction and Commentary*. The Anchor Bible, Volume 37A. William Foxwell Albright and David Noel Freedman, General Editors (New York: Doubleday, 1995), 264.

7. Kurt A. Richardson, *James: An Exegetical and Theological Exposition of Holy Scripture*. The New American Commentary, Volume 36. E. Ray Clendenen, General Editor (Nashville: Broadman and Holman Publishers, 1997), 157.

8. *Ibid.*, 158.

9. THE MARK OF TRUE WISDOM

1. David McCullough, *John Adams* (New York: Simon and Schuster Paperbacks, 2001), 570.

2. *Ibid.*, 571.

3. Peter H. Davids, *James*. New International Biblical Commentary. W. Ward Gasque, New Testament Editor (Peabody, MA: Hendrickson Publishers, Inc., 1989), 88.

4. McCullough, 260.

5. Davids, 90.
6. Jan Karon, *At Home in Mitford* (New York: Penguin Books, 1994), 130.
7. Kurt A. Richardson, *James: an Exegetical and Theological Exposition of Holy Scripture.* The New American Commentary, Volume 36. E. Ray Clendenen, General Editor (Nashville: Broadman and Holman Publishers, 1997), 168.
8. Davids, 90.
9. R. Kent Hughes, *James: Faith That Works.* Preaching the Word (Wheaton, IL: Crossway Books, 1991), 159.
10. *Ibid.*
11. Marie E. Isaacs, *Reading Hebrews and James: A Literary and Theological Commentary.* Reading the New Testament. Charles H. Talbert, General Editor (Macon, GA: Smith and Helwys Publishing, Inc., 2002), 222.
12. *The Book of Common Prayer* (New York: The Seabury Press, 1979), 833.
13. Sophie Laws, *The Epistle of James.* Harper's New Testament Commentaries. Henry Chadwick, General Editor (San Francisco: Harper and Row, Publishers, 1980), 160.
14. *Ibid.*, 163.

10. AN INVITATION TO HEALING

1. Douglas J. Moo, *The Letter of James.* The Pillar New Testament Commentary. D. A. Carson, Series Editor (Grand Rapids, MI: William B. Eerdmans Publishing Company, 2000), 186.
2. David P. Nystrom, *James.* The NIV Application Commentary. Terry Muck, General Editor (Grand Rapids, MI: Zondervan, 1997), 229.
3. R. Kent Hughes, *James: Faith That Works.* Preaching the Word (Wheaton, IL: Crossway Books, 1991), 184.
4. Ralph P. Martin, *James.* Word Biblical Commentary. David A. Hubbard and Glenn W. Barker, General Editors (Waco, TX: Word, 1988), 152.
5. Moo, 194.
6. Martin, 153.
7. Hughes, 184.
8. Martin, 154.
9. *Ibid.*, 155.
10. William Barclay, *The New Daily Study Bible: The Letters of James and Peter.* Linda Foster, Editor (Louisville, KY: Westminster John Knox Press, 2003), 126.
11. *Ibid.*
12. Craig L. Blomberg and Mariam J. Kamell, *James.* Zondervan Exegetical Commentary on the New Testament, Volume 16. Clinton E. Arnold, General Editor (Grand Rapids, MI: Zondervan, 2008), 196.
13. *Ibid.*, 201.

11. ALL THAT WE REALLY HAVE IS NOW

1. N. T. Wright, *The Early Christian Letters for Everyone: James, Peter, John, and Judah.* New Testament for Everyone (Louisville, KY: Westminster John Knox Press, 2011), 30.
2. Dan. G. McCarney, *James.* Baker Exegetical Commentary on the New Testament. Robert W. Yarbrough and Robert H. Stein, Editors (Grand Rapids, MI: Baker Academic, 2009), 220.
3. R. Kent Hughes, *James: Faith That Works.* Preaching the Word (Wheaton, IL: Crossway Books, 1991), 194.
4. *Ibid.*, 195.
5. Peter H. Davids, *James.* New International Biblical Commentary. W. Ward Gasque, New Testament Editor (Peabody, MA: Hendrickson Publishers, Inc., 1989), 104.
6. *Ibid.*
7. Luke Timothy Johnson, "James." *Harper's Bible Commentary.* James L. Mays, General Editor (San Francisco: Harper and Row, Publishers, 1988), 1276.
8. Kurt A. Richardson, *James: An Exegetical and Theological Exposition of Holy Scripture.* The New American Commentary, Volume 36. E. Ray Clendenen, General Editor (Nashville, TN: Broadman and Holman Publishers, 1997), 194.
9. McCartney, 220.
10. Hughes, 196.
11. *Ibid.*, 199.
12. *Ibid.*
13. Sophie Laws, *The Epistle of James.* Harper's New Testament Commentaries. Henry Chadwick, General Editor (San Francisco: Harper and Row, Publishers, 1980), 190.
14. James B. Adamson, *The Epistle of James.* The New International Commentary on the New Testament. F. F. Bruce, Editor (Grand Rapids, MI: William B. Eerdmans Publishing Company, 1976), 181.

12. CARELESS LUXURY

1. R. Kent Hughes, *James: Faith That Works.* Preaching the Word (Wheaton, IL: Crossway Books, 1991), 211.
2. N. T. Wright, *The Early Christian Letters for Everyone: James, Peter, John, and Judah* (Louisville, KY: Westminster John Knox Press, 2011), 35.
3. Luke Timothy Johnson, *The Letter of James: A New Translation with Introduction and Commentary.* The Anchor Bible, Volume 37A. William Foxwell Albright and David Noel Freedman, General Editors (New York: Doubleday, 1995), 308.
4. Luke Timothy Johnson, "James." *Harper's Bible Commentary.* James L. Mays, General Editor (San Francisco: Harper and Row, Publishers, 1988), 1277.

5. Mt 27:57-61; Mk 15:42-47; Lk 23:50-56; Jn 19:38-42.
6. Lk 19:1-10.
7. Acts 16:12-15.
8. Johnson, *The Letter of James: A New Translation with Introduction and Commentary*, 308.
9. Hughes, 216.
10. Craig L. Blomberg and Mariam J. Kamell, *James*. Exegetical Commentary on the New Testament. Clinton E. Arnold, General Editor (Grand Rapids, MI: Zondervan, 2008), 225.
11. *The HarperCollins Study Bible* (New Revised Standard Version). Wayne A. Meeks, General Editor (New York: HarperCollins, Publishers, 1993), 2274.
12. Wright, 36.
13. Ralph P. Martin, *James*. Word Biblical Commentary, Volume 48. David A. Hubbard and Glenn W. Barker, General Editors (Waco, TX: Word, 1988), 183.

13. PATIENCE AND ENDURANCE

1. N. T. Wright, *The Early Christian Letters for Everyone: James, Peter, John and Judah*. New Testament for Everyone (Louisville, KY: Westminster John Knox Press, 2011), 37.
2. *Ibid.*, 38.
3. David P. Nystrom, *The NIV Application Commentary: James*. Terry Muck, General Editor (Grand Rapids, MI: Zondervan, 1997), 284.
4. *Ibid.*, 286.
5. Craig L. Blomberg and Mariam J. Kamell, *James*. Zondervan Exegetical Commentary on the New Testament. Clinton E. Arnold, General Editor (Grand Rapids, MI: Zondervan, 2008), 228.
6. Luke Timothy Johnson, *The Letter of James: A New Translation with Introduction and Commentary*. The Anchor Bible, Volume 37A. William Foxwell Albright and David Noel Freedman, General Editors (New York: Doubleday, 1995), 317.
7. Nystrom, 287.
8. Mt 6:4; cf. Mt 13:57; Lk 4:24.
9. Sophie Laws, *The Epistle of James*. Harper's New Testament Commentaries. Henry Chadwick, General Editor (San Francisco: Harper and Row, Publishers, 1980), 215.
10. Kurt A. Richardson, *James: An Exegetical and Theological Exposition of Holy Scripture*. The New American Commentary, Volume 36. E. Ray Clendenen, General Editor (Nashville: Broadman and Holman Publishers, 1997), 225.
11. Ralph P. Martin, *James*. Word Biblical Commentary, Volume 48. David A. Hubbard and Glenn W. Barker, General Editors (Waco, TX: Word, 1988), 197.

12. William Barclay, *The New Daily Study Bible: The Letters of James and Peter.* Linda Foster, Editor (Louisville, KY: Westminster John Knox Press, 2003), 145.

13. Nystrom, 292.

14. R. Kent Hughes, *James: Faith That Works.* Preaching the Word (Wheaton, IL: Crossway Books, 1991), 235.

15. Wright, 38.

16. Aída Besançon Spencer, *A Commentary on James.* Kregel Exegetical Library (Grand Rapids, MI: Kregel Academic, 2020), 270.

14. A RICH TREASURY OF PRAISE

1. Marie E. Isaacs, *Reading Hebrews and James: A Literary and Theological Commentary.* Reading the New Testament. Charles H. Talbert, General Editor (Macon, GA: Smyth and Helwys Publishing, Inc., 2002), 246.

2. *The Book of Common Prayer* (New York: The Seabury Press, 1979), 856.

3. N. T. Wright, *The Early Christian Letters for Everyone: James, Peter, John, and Judah* (Louisville, KY: Westminster John Knox Press, 2011), 41.

4. R. Kent Hughes, *James: Faith That Works.* Preaching the Word (Wheaton, IL: Crossway Books, 1991), 264.

5. Ralph P. Martin, *James.* Word Biblical Commentary, Volume 48. David A. Hubbard and Glenn W. Barker, General Editors (Waco, TX: Word, 1988), 214.

6. James B. Adamson, *The Epistle of James.* The New International Commentary on the New Testament. F. F. Bruce, Editor (Grand Rapids, MI: William B. Eerdmans Publishing Company, 1976), 197.

7. Martin Kähler, *The So-Called Historical Jesus and the Historic Biblical Christ.* Fortress Texts in Modern Theology. Translated, edited, and with an introduction by Carl E. Braaten (Philadelphia, PA: Fortress Press, 1964), 80.

8. William Barclay, *The New Daily Study Bible: The Letters of James and Peter.* Linda Foster, Editor (Louisville, KY: Westminster John Knox Press, 2003), 148.

9. *Ibid.*, 149.

10. David P. Nystrom, *The NIV Application Commentary: James.* The NIV Application Commentary Series. Terry Muck, General Editor (Grand Rapids, MI: Zondervan, 1997), 310.

11. 1 Thessalonians 5:16-18.

15. A SUMMONS TO ACTION

1. Dan G. McCartney, *James.* Baker Exegetical Commentary on the New Testament. Robert W. Yarbrough and Robert H. Stein, Editors (Grand Rapids, MI: Baker Academic, 2009), 259.

2. Mt 17:1-9; Mk 9:2-10; Lk 9:28-36.

3. Luke Timothy Johnson, *The Letter of James: A New Translation with Introduction and Commentary*. The Anchor Bible, Volume 37A. William Foxwell Albright and David Noel Freedman, General Editors (New York: Doubleday, 1995), 336.

4. Aída Besançon Spencer, *A Commentary on James*. Kregel Exegetical Library (Grand Rapids, MI: Kregel Academic, 2020), 287.

5. Acts 12:17; 15:13; 21:18; 1 Corinthians 15:7; Galatians 2:9.

6. Johnson, 338.

7. *Ibid.*, 345.

8. Ralph P. Martin, *James*. Word Biblical Commentary. David A Hubbard and Glenn W. Barker, General Editors (Waco, TX: Word, 1988), 219.

9. *The HarperCollins Study Bible* (New Revised Standard Version). Wayne A. Meeks, General Editor (New York: HarperCollins, Publishers, 1993), 2273.

10. Pheme Perkins, *First and Second Peter, James, and Jude*. Interpretation: A Bible Commentary for Teaching and Preaching. James Luther Mays, Editor (Louisville, KY: Westminster John Knox Press, 2012), 136.

11. Douglas J. Moo, *The Letter of James* The Pillar New Testament Commentary. D. A. Carson, General Editor (Grand Rapids, MI: William B. Eerdmans Publishing Company, 2000), 248.

12. *Ibid.*, 249.

13. Martin, 221.

14. Johnson, 346.

BIBLIOGRAPHY

Adamson, James B. *The Epistle of James*. The New International Commentary on the New Testament. F. F. Bruce, Editor. Grand Rapids, MI: William B. Eerdmans Publishing Company, 1976.

Andria, Solomon. "James." *Africa Bible Commentary*. Tokunboh Adeyemo, General Editor. Grand Rapids, MI: Zondervan, 2006.

Barclay, William. *The New Daily Study Bible: The Letters of James and Peter*. Linda Foster, Editor. Louisville, KY: Westminster John Knox Press, 2003.

Blomberg, Craig L., and Mariam J. Kamell. *James*. Zondervan Exegetical Commentary on the New Testament, Volume 16. Clinton E. Arnold, General Editor. Grand Rapids, MI: Zondervan, 2008.

The Book of Common Prayer. New York: The Seabury Press, 1979.

Davids, Peter H. *James.* New International Biblical Commentary. W. Ward Gasque, New Testament Editor. Peabody, MA: Hendrickson Publishers, Inc., 1989.

The HarperCollins Study Bible (New Revised Standard Version). Wayne A. Meeks, General Editor. New York: HarperCollins, Publishers, Inc., 1993.

Holladay, Carl R. *Introduction to the New Testament.* Reference Edition. Waco, TX: Baylor University Press, 2017.

Hughes, R. Kent. *James: Faith That Works.* Preaching the Word. Wheaton, IL: Crossway Books, 1991.

Isaacs, Marie E. *Reading Hebrews and James: A Literary and Theological Commentary.* Reading the New Testament. Charles H. Talbert, General Editor. Macon, GA: Smyth and Helwys Publishing, Inc., 2002.

Johnson, Luke Timothy. *"James." Harper's Bible Commentary.* James L. Mays, General Editor. San Francisco: Harper and Row, Publishers, 1988.

____. *The Letter of James: A New Translation with Introduction and Commentary.* The Anchor Bible, Volume 37A. William Foxwell Albright and David Noel Freedman, General Editors. New York: Doubleday, 1995.

Kähler, Martin. *The So-Called Historical Jesus and the Historic Biblical Christ.* Fortress Texts in Modern Theology. Translated, edited, and with an introduction by Carl E. Braaten. Philadelphia, PA: Fortress Press, 1964.

Karon, Jan. *At Home in Mitford.* New York: Penguin Books, 1994.

Keats, John. Letter to George and Georgiana Keats. February 14, 1918.

Laws, Sophie. *The Epistle of James.* Harper's New Testament Commentaries. Henry Chadwick, General Editor. San Francisco: Harper and Row, Publishers, 1980.

___. *"The Letter of James."* *The HarperCollins Study Bible* (New Revised Standard Version). Wayne A. Meeks, General Editor. New York: HarperCollins, Publishers, Inc., 1993.

Martin, Ralph P. *James.* Word Biblical Commentary. David A. Hubbard and Glenn W. Barker, General Editors. Waco, TX: Word, 1988.

McCartney, Dan G. *James.* Baker Exegetical Commentary on the New Testament. Robert W. Yarbrough and Robert H. Stein, Editors. Grand Rapids, MI: Baker Academic, 2009.

McCullough, David. *John Adams.* New York: Simon and Schuster Paperbacks, 2001.

Moo, Douglas J. *The Letter of James.* The Pillar New Testament Commentary. D. A. Carson, General Editor. Grand Rapids, MI: William B. Eerdmans Publishing Company, 2000.

Nystrom, David P. *James.* The NIV Application Commentary. Terry Muck, General Editor. Grand Rapids, MI: Zondervan, 1997.

Perkins, Pheme. *First and Second Peter, James and Jude.* Interpretation: A Bible Commentary for Teaching and Preaching. James Luther Mays, Editor. Louisville, KY: Westminster John Knox Press, 2012.

Richardson, Kurt A. *James: An Exegetical and Theological Exposition of Holy Scripture.* The New American Commentary, Volume 36. E. Ray Clendenen, General Editor. Nashville: Broadman and Holman Publishers, 1997.

Webster's Ninth New Collegiate Dictionary. Springfield, MA: Merriam-Webster, Inc., Publishers, 1987.

Wright, N. T. *The Early Christian Letters for Everyone: James, Peter, John, and Judah.* New Testament for Everyone. Louisville, KY: Westminster John Knox Press, 2011.

ABOUT THE AUTHOR

Joel W. Huffstetler is Rector of St. Luke's Episcopal Church in Cleveland, Tennessee. Ordained in 1990, he previously served as Assistant to the Rector of St. Paul's Episcopal Church, Chattanooga, Tennessee, and as Rector of St. Andrew's Episcopal Church in Canton, North Carolina. He is the author or editor of twelve books and numerous articles and reviews.

Made in the USA
Coppell, TX
15 January 2022

71558932R00080